Getaway GUIDE

THE
Kruger
National
PARK

CAMERON EWART-SMITH

SUNBIRD
PUBLISHERS

SUNBIRD
PUBLISHERS

First edition 2005
Second edition 2007
Third edition 2009

Sunbird Publishers (Pty) Ltd
2nd Floor, Design Centre, 179 Loop Street
Cape Town, 8001

www.sunbirdpublishers.co.za

Registration number: 1984/003543/07

Design and layout: Megan Knox
Cartographer: John Hall
Editor: Sean Fraser
Editorial adviser: David Bristow
Updated: David Bristow
Production: Marje Hemp and Andrew de Kock

Reproduction by Resolution Colour, Cape Town
Printed by Star Standard Industries (Pte) Ltd, Singapore

ISBN 978-1-920289-08-9

PHOTOGRAPH CREDITS: (l=left; r=right; t=top; b=bottom; m=middle)
Photography by **Cameron Ewart-Smith**, with the exception of those listed below:
David Bristow: 1, 3, 4, 5, 18, 19r, 23, 25t, 27b, 38tr, 41, 46t, 51r, 53, 57b, 59, 63b, 69, 70l, 74t, 77, 90t, 91, 97b, 100l, 101b,
103, 110t, 110b, 116, 127, 132t, 160, 161, 162, 168 (main pic), 169r, 176, 190, 201, 202. **Robyn Daly**: 64, 83b, 129, 187. **Justin
Fox**: cover bl & bm, 22, 67t, 195, 205b. **Peter Frost**: 186. **Rob House**: cover 1 & bm. **Cathy Lanz**: 44b. **Don Pinnock**:
138 (main pic); 159. **David Rogers**: 25b, 108, 130b, 131, 134l, 198. **David Steele**: 60b, 74b, 76r, 83t, 86, 88t, 156 (main
pic), 188, 193, 199. **Patrick Wagner**: 1, 97t, 99, 111, 124t, 196. **Photo Access: HPH Photography** 13, 189, D Allen 40t, F
Hodson 52, Steve Vincent 56, James Stevenson-Hamilton 182.

In Memory

Dick Wilkins 1945 to 2005

Dick's vision, passion and drive gave birth to many of the finest wildlife books in South Africa. He was particularly fond of Kruger – his favourite refuge from the frenetic world of books. Dick, as founder of Sunbird Publishers, I hope this guide meets with your approval.

Acknowledgements

First and foremost, thanks to Marjorie Hemp at *Getaway*, without your Herculean effort this book would have remained in limbo. Also thanks to David Bristow, your editorial advice and the countless additions and suggestions truly transformed this work. Sean Fraser, my editor, spent his last moments as a single guy editing and reworking this text, leaving his post only – literally – as the church organ began to play. His efforts transformed chaos into order. Thanks too to designer Megan Knox for refusing to accept off-mustard as a colour! All the folk at Sunbird Publishers and in particular Natanya Mulholland, who took over the reins from Dick Wilkins under very trying circumstances – and cracked them good and hard – thanks. A special mention must go to SANParks chief, David Mabunda, and at Kruger William Mbasa, Sinna Mphatse and all the rangers, guides and managers who accommodated me and gave so freely of their knowledge – keep up the good work, I think Kruger rocks! Raymond Travers in particular went something like the extra 10 miles in helping to update and correct the new editions. Thanks Lesley Sutton and **Land Rover** who provided me with a vehicle for the duration of my research. Thanks also to James Stevenson-Hamilton for permission to use pictures from the family collection. To my family, thanks for all the support during the production of this book. Last and by no means least, thanks Justine for so much more than simply giving me the freedom to follow my dreams.

Foreword

Over the past 111 years, the Kruger National Park has become a template of conservation and tourism best practice in protected area management for the world. It has become a regular destination for some and an object of considerable passion for most. Within the borders of this two million hectare protected area, its impressive biodiversity and associated cultural heritage continue to thrive thanks to the protection afforded by a proud corps of rangers, backed up by scientists, law enforcers and administration staff.

Unlike in the past, it reaches out to neighbouring rural communities with life-changing scholarships, business opportunities and other mutual agreements Since the early 1990s, management philosophy has shifted from concerns around species in ecosystems, to ensuring the whole ecosystem functions as a healthy unit. As implied above, we are now increasingly looking at the park part of a wider landscape mosaic with which we interact on social, economic and of course environmental levels within South Africa's present body politic.

We stive to maintain or create healthy connections via the rivers, the landscape buffer zones and the natural corridors that make us part of a bigger and more sustainable region, which includes efforts to stretch conservation across our borders in the form of the Great Limpopo Transfrontier Park and the neighbouring private nature reserves on the Western boundary.

Even the iconic elephant population has received a new holistic 'face', with a number of possible management options tailored to particular situations, values, park objectives and regional impacts. We believe all this makes Kruger more resilient and dynamic. And we need Kruger to be resilient, to continue in its role as one of the world's conservation icons where people from all over the world can witness the true African wilderness and enjoy accommodation ranging from a camp site to a luxury five-star lodge, all in one park.

My plea to you is that you appreciate and enjoy this park for what it is, a beautiful place where you can experience South Africa's rich Biodiversity without leaving the comfort and safety of your vehicle.

Yours in conservation,
Dr David Mabunda
Chief Executive, SANParks

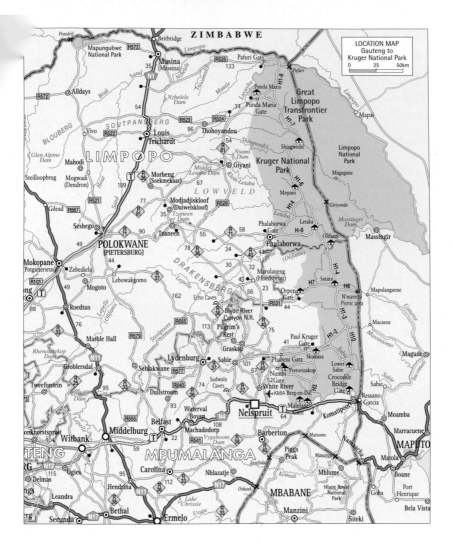

KEY FOR MAPS ON PAGES 35, 45, 55, 61, 68, 75, 91, 103, 117, 123 & 135

Excellent route inside park	Picnic spot
Good route inside park	River and water hole
H12 — Tarred road and number	Park gate
S144 — Gravel road and number	645 ▲ Spot height

Please see page 221 for key to symbols on camp layouts

KEY

Motorway	
National road	
Main road	
Secondary road	tarred untarred
Route numbers	N1 R71 R555
Toll route	T
Distances in kilometres	● 12 ●30 18 ●
Railway	
International boundary	
Provincial boundary	
Nature reserve	Makuya N.R.
River, marsh and dam	
Built-up area	
Secondary town	O
Small town	◉
Large village	◎
Village	○
Small village or station	○
International airport	✈
Rest camp / holiday resort	⌂

Kruger National Park

Entrance gate	ᕒ
Main camp	⌂
Private camp / Bush lodge	⌂
Bushveld camp	✻
Tented and caravan camps	△⌂
Spot height	▲535
No entry	⊖
Picnic spot	Ⓟ
Lookout point	☀
Border crossing	✕ Beitbridge
Place of interest	✶Baobab Tree
Monument / memorial / plaque	⬛
Cave	⌒
Waterfall	⥾
Hot spring	:Υ:

Vegetation

Sandveld, Sour Lowveld Bush / Arid Mountain Bush	
Mopane Bushveld	
Mopane Shrubveld	
Riverine Forest / Bush	
Sweet Lowveld Bushveld	
Lebombo Arid Mtn Bushveld	
Mixed Lowveld Bushveld	
Sour Lowveld Bushveld	

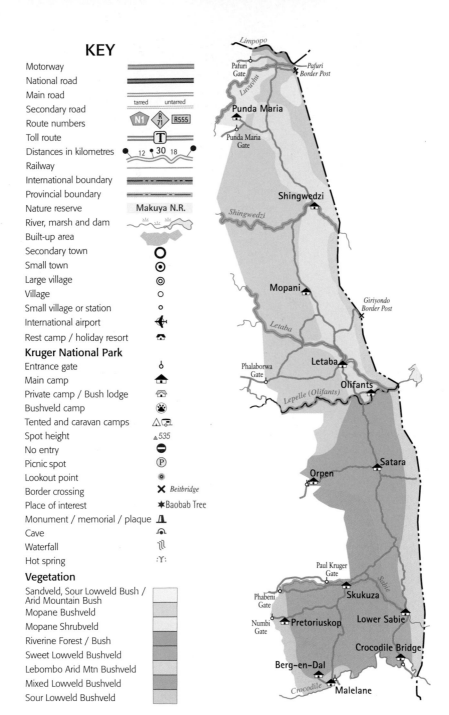

Contents

How to use this book

The *Getaway Guide to the Kruger National Park* is organised into four parts:

Planning a visit (chapters 1 to 3): A host of background and planning information including how to make reservations, health considerations, what to pack and what to expect when arriving at the gate.

Where to stay and what to do (chapters 4 to 26): Detailed information on each rest camp, including facilities, best drives and activities on offer, as well as details on all the private concessions, 4x4 trails, walking safaris and other activities.

What makes Kruger tick (chapters 27 to 29): Background reading on the park, including the geology, history, weather systems and ecological functioning.

Kruger at a glance: A directory of useful contact details. Enables you to find critical information on camps, gate times, distance, useful contacts and so on … at a glance.

KEY TO CAMP INFORMATION

Under each camp in 'Where to stay' the following information is given:
• The contact number of the camp
• The facilities on offer
• The nearest entrance gate

A wheelchair-friendly rating
* = poor; ** = need assistance; *** = doable, but with assistance needed in places; **** = very limited assistance required; ***** = plain sailing.

KEY TO CAMP MAPS IS ON PAGE 6.

Introduction

"If our lives are dominated by a search for happiness, then perhaps few activities reveal as much about the dynamics of this quest – in all its ardour and paradoxes – than our travels. They express, however inarticulately, an understanding of what life might be about, outside the constraints of work and the struggle for survival."

Alain de Botton in *The Art of Travel*.

The Kruger National Park is not only one of the world's greatest game reserves, but one of its iconic tourist attractions. It stretches more than 500 kilometres along South Africa's northeastern border with Mozambique and currently encompasses nearly two million hectares of primal Africa. This offers visitors an opportunity to glimpse history – opening a window to a time before this magnificent continent was systematically sacrificed on the altar of human progress. Few guests pass its gates today without experiencing a true emotional tie to Mother Earth as it once was.

Kruger is not a glorified tourist trap, but a true conservation showcase – there has been no need to invent oversized cartoon-mouse attractions here. Within its fences, ecosystems function much as they always have, with the exception of a little human tinkering here and there. The park is home to a plethora of plant and animal species interacting in a delicate web strung between two well-defined climatic zones and 14 distinct ecozones. There are few places in the world today that can compete bio-

My former boss once told me of his first journey into the park as a kid. His father, who coincidentally was also on his first visit, was understandably excited at the prospect of showing this untamed wonderland to his young family. Soon after entering the gate they encountered a small herd of impala on the side of the road. Excited, dad stopped the car, switched off the engine, and leaning over the seat for emphasis quietly whispered à la David Attenborough: "Wow, kids, look at that. Isn't that magnificent? You might not see a sight like that again...."

logically; and few parks offer anything close to the diversity of large mammals, which the average visitor to Kruger can tick in a couple of days.

Possibly the greatest challenge the park has overcome in recent times, however, has been the shift from an overly protectionist, non-economically viable management style to one where visitor needs and wants are accommodated, but without compromising conservation initiatives.

Where once Kruger Park was totally reliant on government handouts for survival, it now stands on its own financially secure feet, offering an exciting range of activities and broad range of accommodation options – from humble camp sites to award-winning luxury, private lodges. Through these initiatives Kruger has realised its potential and indeed realises handsome profits, which directly fund conservation initiatives not only within the park but across South Africa.

Most importantly, Kruger today has shrugged off its apartheid-era past of forced removals and colour segregated amenities. Where once animals took precedence over people there are now exciting conservation–community partnerships – such as the Makuleke concession in the north of the park – which are critical for the ongoing success of conservation. The park's gates are open to all, rest camp units are being upgraded to 3* and 4* standard, and entrance gates have new facilities – a place all South African, can look to with pride. These days Kruger is not only a park of animals, but a park for the people ... where visitors can find peace and tranquillity from the urban jungle that constitutes most of our busy lives.

It's hoped that this book will aid you in your quest to see Africa as it once was, while enabling you to understand a little more of what you find. Enjoy your visit and remember to take the time to smell the bushveld and let your senses absorb your surroundings.

THE GREATER LIMPOPO TRANSFRONTIER PARK

These days Kruger has taken on an even greater significance. With a long history of careful management and protection, it has escaped the ravages of poaching and human encroachment that have disastrously affected many similar reserves in neighbouring countries. Consequently, the park is able to render assistance in restocking other seriously denuded areas as the Peace Parks initiative gains momentum.

This bold plan aims to drop border fences between adjacent wildlife reserves in neighbouring countries, in order to create huge swathes of land under careful conservation. This should alleviate some of the overstocking problems reserves such as Kruger are experiencing, while returning wildlife to areas previousloy depleted of wildlife. Peace Parks will not only benefit game, but will also provide an effective vehicle for economic empowerment in neighbouring communities particularly hard hit by poverty.

The Greater Limpopo Transfrontier Park is the amalgam of Kruger, Gonarezhou National Park in Zimbabwe and the Limpopo National Park in Mozambique and covers an area of 3,5 million hectares. The first tangible stage in the creation of this transfrontier park has been the dropping of border fences that were put up between Mozambique and South Africa.

Planning your visit

"The caravan was not an imposing one under the circumstances. A light wagon, drawn by six emaciated oxen weakened by long and exhausting transport work under active service conditions; three good ponies ...; a [lad] named Nicholas as general factotum; a Sotho youth from the Orange Free State as horse attendant; a driver and leader for the wagon [and] finally a quaint old native known as 'Toothless Jack'..." James Stevenson-Hamilton on his arrival in the park, from *South African Eden: The Kruger National Park.*

The Masorini Archaeological Site (left) and roan antelope (right) are both worth considering when planning your visit to the park.

The Kruger National Park has some of the best facilities of any park in Africa, which for the price makes it one of the best 'value for money' destinations of its kind anywhere in the world. The park has evolved tremendously from its earliest beginnings – back in the early 1900s – when visitors were pretty much left to fend for themselves. These days, the intricate road network is excellent and you don't require bush survival skills to get about. The park's camps and lodges, restaurants, camping sites and ablutions are spotless, and the staff friendly and helpful. All the rest camps are equipped with electricity (220 V), and all units except safari tents have air-conditioning. Fridges, bedding, towels and soap are supplied in your chalet, although in some cases cutlery and crockery need to be hired – it's advisable to check on this when you make your booking. The larger rest camps have shops, restaurants, autobank facilities or cash machines, swimming pools and emergency facilities. If you plan to camp, or opt to stay in the safari tents, you may have to share communal ablution facilities. Full details are given in the rest camp descriptions.

Visitor entertainment has also undergone immense changes and a host of new, exciting activities, such as night drives, guided bushwalks, bush braais and breakfasts and more are offered by all rest camps. This chapter will help you plan your trip in order to make the most of your visit and aims to answer any of those nagging questions you may have, whether you're a first time visitor, haven't visited the park for ages or are an old Kruger regular.

Making a booking

All bookings for Kruger (and all other national parks, for that matter) are made with SANParks Central Reservations in Tshwane (Pretoria) on phone 012-428-9111, mobile 082-233-9111 or e-mail reservations@sanparks.org. Check the 'real time' booking facility (accommodation and activities) on South African National Parks' website at www.sanparks.org.

Bookings are taken up to 11 months in advance for any of the park facilities, while last-minute adjustments (i.e. after you've arrived in the park) to these existing bookings can be made with the camp receptionists who will assist you where possible.

SANPARKS SATELLITE RESERVATION OFFICES
Johannesburg: 011-678-8870
Cape Town: 021-487-6800
Durban: 031-304-4934
Nelspruit: 013-755-1988

Paul Kruger's Statue at Kruger Gate.

Kruger offers a diverse range of activities such as mountain biking at Olifants Camp.

Where to stay

Kruger has 11 rest camps, five bush camps, seven satellite camps and 15 private lodges offering a wide selection of accommodation as diverse as its ecosystems. You can find something to fit just about any pocket, from inexpensive camp sites to luxurious private safari lodges.

The south and central regions of the park boast numerous camps, accommodating the many visitors drawn by the incredible numbers of predators and large herds of antelopes that occur here. The northern region tends to be quieter as there are generally fewer animals and, consequently, fewer visitors, but camps such as Punda Maria nevertheless have their own special character and suite of attractions.

Planning your itinerary

One day If you are a day visitor or have only one night, head to the southern region (page 32) and follow the H4-1 between Skukuza and Lower Sabie.

This road is one of the busiest in the park but not without reason as game is prolific, and ticking the Big Five and more is relatively common along this route. Alternatively head for the central region (page 72) through the Orpen Gate (page 73) and drive the routes around Satara (page 78). If you are an avid birder, enter the park at Pafuri Gate and take the drive to Crook's Corner (page 136), which offers some of the best birding in South Africa.

Two to four days If you have only a limited amount of time available – say two or three days – or are mainly concerned with seeing the Big Five, head for the southern (page 32) or central regions (page 72) of the park. These teem with game and have the highest density of predators. It is also worth staying in one or at most two camps; that way you get familiar with the surroundings and don't waste time packing and unpacking as you move between camps.

Five days and more This allows you

greater flexibility. It is worth ...ding a night or two in the northern ...gion (page 114) for the birds, specials ...uch as tsessebe and eland, huge buffalo herds as well as for big trees, before moving south. Spend a night or two in the central region (page 72) around Satara where plains game such as zebra and wildebeest and predators such as lion and cheetah are regularly sighted, before entering the southern region (page 32), which is probably the most game-rich region in the park.

What to pack

Depending on which accommodation you choose, you may simply need a few things for your vehicle, as most of the rest camps are fully equipped and have basic shops, restaurants and take-aways – check the 'Where to stay' section (pages 31–137) for the facilities offered at each camp. Towels and soap are provided in all units.

If you are camping you will need tents, mattresses, cooking utensils (and if you're my mother-in-law, a portable kitchen sink too). Also, take an extension cable and adaptor for the caravan plugs (available from most good camping stores.)

Typically, you will be spending many hours in your vehicle, unless you are staying in one of the private concession lodges, or are using a tour operator. Take a cooler box that you can access without getting out the car. An additional cooler box, into which you can pack meat and other perishables when moving between camps, is also really useful.

During the day, temperatures are

Water is safe to drink in all the rest camps, unless you are specifically informed otherwise by reception.

CHECKLIST
Cooler boxes
Kids' amusements – games, books, swimming costumes and so on
Sun protection – hat, sunglasses, sunscreen
Mosquito repellent
Camera
Binoculars
Guidebooks to the fauna and flora
First-aid kit

pleasantly warm to hot year round, with few exceptions – make sure you have hats, sunblock and sunglasses. Pack a swimming costume, as most larger camps have swimming pools. Take cool, long clothes for the evenings, which help prevent mozzie bites but don't leave you drenched in sweat.

Pack something warm, even in summer, as chilly nights are always possible and particularly so if you plan to take night drives in the park's open game-viewing vehicles.

In winter, warm gear is essential for night drives and early morning starts.

It's worth taking your basic first-aid kit – with antihistamine cream or spray (such as Stingose), plasters, headache tablets and so on.

Most importantly, don't forget to take binoculars (8x35 or 10x25 are recommended). Ideally, everyone in your car should have their own pair; failing that, try to have a pair between two.

Keen photographers will need the longest lens they can afford and loads of film or memory sticks (I usually work out what I think I'll need and then double it for Kruger).

A number of excellent maps, short guides and animal reference books are available, which will enhance your visit (see 'Game drives with kids' on page 27 for more info on kids' products and the suggested reading list). Most importantly, a concise guide to the animals and a bird book are the first things I pack once my camera gear is all in. I would be lost without them....

There and away

By air Fly into Kruger–Mpumalanga International Airport outside Nelspruit or to Phalaborwa with SA Airlink, from where you can hire a car, meet your pre-arranged tours or catch a transfer flight into Skukuza Airport (scheduled to re-open 'soon'). Most car-hire companies have offices at the airport (see 'Useful contacts' on page 219 for car hire at Skukuza).
By car There are 10 gates into Kruger, allowing visitors some flexibility in their itineraries. Plan to arrive at the gates with enough time to reach your over-night camp. There are stiff fines arriving late, but you can pre-organi an escort for a fee.

Numbi (411 km from Johannesburg), Phabeni (440 km) and Paul Kruger (460 km) gates are little over 5½ hours from Johannesburg along good tar roads. The quickest route is the N4 toll road east from Gauteng through Witbank, Belfast and Nelspruit.

The Malelane (428 km, 6 hrs) and Crocodile Bridge (475 km, 6½ hrs) gates are Kruger's southernmost gates, reached by following the N4 toll road mentioned above through Nelspruit towards Komatipoort.

Phalaborwa (490 km, 6 hrs) and Orpen (490 km, 6 hrs) gates are centrally situated allowing access to the central regions of the park. To reach Phalaborwa Gate, take the N4 east from Gauteng turning north onto the R540 at the Belfast/Dullstroom turn-off and follow this through Dullstroom, Lydenburg, Hoedspruit and Phalaborwa. From Hoedspruit you can turn south on the R40 towards Klaserie and the Orpen Gate. To reach the Orpen Gate from the south, continue along the N4 to Nelspruit and then take the R538 north through White River, Hazyview and Bushbuckridge, continuing north on the R40 towards Klaserie and turning east onto the R531 a few kilometres from the town.

Punda Maria (550 km, 7 hrs) and Pafuri Gate (600 km, 8 hrs) are Kruger's northernmost gates, reached by following the N1 toll road north through Tshwane (Pretoria), Polokwane (Pietersburg) and Louis Trichardt. For Punda Maria turn onto the R524 in

Zebra wade through the thick, green grass typical of summer near Lower Sabie.

Louis Trichardt towards Thohoyandou; for Pafuri continue 54 km north from Louis Trichardt and turn east onto the R525. Both the R524 and R525 are good tar roads although you will not achieve the 120 km an hour speed of the N1 as these are narrower and, particularly in the case of the R524, well populated semi-rural roads.

When to go

Kruger is great year round. Many people prefer the winter months when the temperatures are cooler, no rain is expected, the vegetation is less thick and there is less risk of malaria.

During school holidays in April, July and December and over long weekends accommodation can be difficult to obtain and the number of day visitors increases. It's best to book ahead or visit at a less crowded time.

Summer: November to March The park is very hot and humid, often with dramatic thundershowers. Consequent-ly, the vegetation is lush and game is often difficult to spot. On hot days animals are more active in the early mornings and late afternoons so make an early start.

Autumn: March to May Rainfall is usually highest and temperatures are still hot. Vegetation is at its thickest. On the plus side, many of the antelope species are in their rut season, which makes fascinating viewing as males battle over territories.

Winter: May to August The climate is very pleasant with lovely warm days, although nights can be chilly. The vegetation is less thick and game tends to congregate near permanent water, making game viewing easier.

Spring: August to October Possibly the best of all seasons to visit. Many migrant birds return; the vegetation has not yet become overgrown and the animals remain congregated near permanent water sources ... particularly if the previous year was a dry one.

On arrival 2

Try to arrive at the gates of the park as early as possible so as to get through the formalities without rushing and enjoy a leisurely game drive on your way to your rest camp.

At the gate, report to reception (left), where you will be issued with a permit. After a few formalities (top left) you will be free to enjoy the park (above).

At the gate

Report to reception with your booking form, where you will be issued with an entry permit. This is checked at every rest camp and when you leave the park, so don't lose it. If you need to leave the park for the day and plan to return, ask for a re-entry stamp on this permit. This allows you to re-enter the park free and without having to report at reception.

CONSERVATION FEES

Historically, SANParks charged a once-off entry fee for access to its parks. However, due to the need to generate ecotourism and transfrontier park income, this changed in mid-2003 to a daily conservation fee. South African citizens and members of SADC countries (Angola, Botswana, Democratic Republic of Congo (DRC), Lesotho, Malawi, Mauritius, Mozambique, Namibia, Seychelles, South Africa, Swaziland, Tanzania, Zambia and Zimbabwe) pay reduced fees. Check current fees on www.sanparks.org (/parks/kruger/tourism/tariffs). There are also pensioner concessions. They can be paid in advance or at each rest camp when you check in.

WILD CARDS

The Wild Card is a loyalty programme aimed at facilitating affordable access to all national parks for South Africans, SADC citizens and international visitors. Members enjoy free access (i.e. no daily conservation fees) to a specific cluster of national parks and, where applicable, provincial or private reserves. Cards are available at all national parks and certain tourism-related venues through-

Above: Phalaborwa entrance gate.
Opposite: Pretoriuskop restaurant.

out the country.

International visitors pay a higher fee and are eligible for only the 'All Clusters' option, which allows access to all national parks and Cape Nature Conservation properties.

In camp

On arrival, report to reception where the receptionists will check your entry permit, charge you for any outstanding fees, issue you with a camp map and direct you to your bungalow, safari tent or camp site.

This is a good time to check the activities currently on offer, ask other visitors about their sightings and check the day's game sighting maps. If there are rangers about, ask them about the area: they have immense knowledge of recent, local animal activity, which can be helpful.

Shopping

Most of the larger rest camps have small shops, which supply a collection of basic foodstuffs, souvenirs, reading material, camera film and so on (see individual camp descriptions and 'Kruger at a glance' (page 212) for those camps with shops). If you are planning on self-catering, particularly in any of the smaller camps, it is advisable to bring the lion's share (excuse the pun) into the park as the stores tend to be a little expensive. The shops do, however, cater for most unfussy eaters. In practice, it works well to supplement your supplies from home with fresh goodies – such as bread, frozen meat, a few veggies, cold drinks, biltong, beer, spirits and popular wines and so on – from the rest camp shops. If you are particular about your toiletries, make sure you bring sufficient for the duration of the trip, as the choice tends to be limited.

Banks There is only one 'full-service' bank in the park, located at Skukuza. However, most larger camps have ATMs – see individual camp descriptions and 'Kruger at a glance' (page 212) – or smaller cash machines where you can get cash advances on your credit or debit card.

Fuel All the larger camps – see individual camp descriptions and 'Kruger at a glance' (page 212) – sell both unleaded and leaded petrol, diesel, oil, brake fluid, fix punctures and will try to assist with minor mechanical difficulties.

I find that there is just so much braaivleis I can stomach, so I tend to spoil myself every couple of days with a meal in one of the restaurants. My five favourites are the Selati Grillhouse in Skukuza and the restaurants at Pretoriuskop, Shingwedzi, Letaba and Lower Sabie rest camps.

Eating out

Kruger is one of the last bastions of braaivleis and most people will choose to chuck a slab of meat onto the fire, while their kids run around on the grassy lawns, or to engage the neighbours in a game of cricket over relaxing in the camp restaurant. Almost every accommodation unit and camp site in the park is equipped with a braai place and discussing the day's sightings with the neighbours while you turn the chops is perhaps the park's most enduring and endearing tradition.

That said, eating out has much to recommend it. Most of the restaurants are modern facilities, or they are in the

...g revamped, and offer ...t spread for a reasonable ...t's more, eating out means ...e in your party is on holiday.

...you are not intending cooking ...yourself at all, be aware that not all camps have restaurants. The quick reference to camp facilities (page 212) indicates which do and more information on these can be found under the respective rest camp descriptions.

Bush braais and breakfasts

SANParks now offers two new eating adventures in conjunction with Compass Game Park Services: bush breakfasts and bush braais. These consist of a game drive into a remote corner of the park, followed by a splendid meal – your traditional braai for dinner,

Fry-up breakfast Kruger style.

and a good ol' fry-up for breakfast – in the unfenced wilds of Africa.

You can book your bush dining adventure while making your reservation or when you arrive in camp; simply contact the receptionist or the restaurant manager.

Health and safety

Visiting Kruger poses a few dangers to your health. The entire park is in a medium- to low-risk malarial area. Further, most camps are remotely situated and with the exception of Skukuza, have little or no medical facilities other than rudimentary first aid.

Malaria This is most prevalent in the wet summer months; in winter, the climate is cooler and drier and hence the incidence of malaria is lower.

Children younger than two years old, pregnant women and people who are suffering from pre-existing medical conditions requiring heavy doses of medication are particularly at risk from malaria and therefore should take special care. If this applies to you, you should consider restricting your visits to the winter months, or to the higher area surrounding Pretoriuskop camp where malaria is less prevalent.

It's advisable to consult your doctor at least two weeks before your visit to the park for advice on which of the prophylactics available is most suitable for you. Alternatively contact one of the travel clinics listed in 'Useful contacts' on page 219. Moreover, minimise mosquito bites on warm summer evenings by wearing long, cool clothing and by using an insect repellent spray or lotion (e.g. Tabard, Peaceful Sleep).

Don't miss guided evening bushwalks, but do take precautions against ticks.

Citronella soap and candles also help. Most units have mosquito netting on the doors and windows. Remember certain strains of malaria are resistant to all prophylactics and so these basic precautions should be taken even if you're taking something.

Should you develop any flu-like symptoms after arriving home, especially within the first month or two, consult your doctor, informing them you have been in a malarial area and insist on the appropriate tests. If you are spending a large amount of time in the park, malarial test kits are available from your nearest travel clinic. If caught early, the cure for malaria should be relatively quick and easy. **Ticks** Unless you are participating in one of the walking trails, or guided bushwalks offered by the park, ticks will not affect you. If you are walking, it helps to wear long pants and to spray your legs and the turn-ups of your pants with an insect repellent. In addition, check carefully on your return, or when you shower in the evening, that no tiny pepper ticks have bypassed the chemical deterrents. These carry a bug, which strikes about 10 days after you've been bitten, making you feel terrible for a week or so. The symptoms are much like those of malaria or flu – high temperature, headache, body ache and tiredness: usually there is a significant welt where the tick bite occurred. It is advisable to seek medical help as soon as you feel the first symptoms as most cases respond well to treatment with antibiotics.

Poisonous snakes and dangerous animals There is little to no chance of you being attacked by snakes or any other animal while you are in the park, as long as you obey the rules, use common sense and do not get out of your

FEVER TREES AND MALARIA

When the first Europeans began moving into tropical Africa they often camped on riverbanks near stands of *Acacia xanthophloea*, the tall, yellow-barked acacias commonly known as fever trees. Invariably, many trekkers developed fevers on the road and consequently blamed the tree and its flowers for their malaise. It was only many years later that the malaria parasite *Plasmodium* sp. was identified, and it became clear that this was transmitted by mosquitoes. The tree was blameless but the common name, fever tree, persists.

car. Snakes do sometimes slither into the rest camps but rarely pose any danger. If you do encounter a snake, report this to reception so that the intruder can be peacefully removed.

At night, you must wear shoes and use a torch as there is a chance that you may meet a snake or step on a scorpion which, although seldom – if ever – fatal, can be very painful.

Frail visitors Most camps are far from medical facilities and you can expect significant delays before medical help arrives. However, don't let this put older or frail visitors off visiting the park, as, in many ways, driving around Kruger is an ideal 'outside' activity requiring little or no physical effort other than finding a comfortable seat in the car. If you are concerned, do not travel too far from Skukuza, which has a resident doctor, dentist and nursing facilities.

Physically challenged visitors Kruger, as with all of South Africa's national parks, is well on the road to becoming wheelchair friendly. Camp managers will assist wherever possible to accommodate physically challenged visitors' needs. It is advisable to check whether any special facilities you require are available (such as baths or ramps) when making your reservation. In addition, where appropriate in this guidebook a star rating has been given (following those given by an internal report by a physically challenged member of SANParks' staff) to facilities indicating their wheelchair friendliness: * is a real struggle; ***** is a breeze.

Deep vein thrombosis These are clots that develop in the veins with nasty repercussions. There are a number of causes, but one exacerbating factor is sitting for many hours – such as cramped in the back seat of a small car on a game drive – which is why it could be an issue for Kruger visitors.

Drinking sufficient fluids, moving your feet, stretching where possible and alighting from your vehicle at designated spots such as views and picnic areas will help (and not only with thrombosis).

Cellphones

Cellphone coverage varies in the park, being confined to camps with some spillover (this is in line with guest surveys). Vodacom generally has the widest coverage. All the networks cover most of the main camps, although you may have to walk around to find a spot that receives a signal. Emergency calls are permitted across networks.

Out & about

3

With over 2500 kilometres of roads to explore, walking trails, 4x4 adventure trails and even mountain
biking trails, Kruger is alive with activities for you to
enjoy on your visit.

Above: Don't miss the opportunity of encountering nocturnal animals on a night drive.
Top: Stop off at the Kruger Tablets on the H1-2 north of Skukuza.

Driving etiquette

Slow, slower ... slowest is the best way to see the park. Things 'pop up' around corners, usually when you least expect it. If you're going too fast you scare the animals and indeed may drive past without seeing them if they are in the bush next to the road. Speed limits on tar are 50 kilometres an hour and on dirt 40 kilometres an hour. Try ambling along at 25 kilometres an hour for really great sightings.

Approach all stationary cars carefully and treat their sighting with respect. The rule is, first in has priority, but be generous. Nothing is more infuriating than when you have a great sighting and someone drives up at speed and parks a vehicle in your line of sight. Equally, if you're first on a scene that has limited 'viewing room', try to park so that other cars will be able to get a sight. Also, do not block the roads as others may not find your first impala sighting as interesting and will want to get past. Report transgressions to The Emergency Call Centre, 013-735-4325, especially private tour guides who force their way into sightings (take the plate number or company name).

Be kind to the bugs, dung beetles and tortoises on the road!

Watching animals

All animals are sensitive to noise and sudden movements. When you see something, it is best to approach slowly, turn off your radio if you've been listening to it, and possibly even your engine allowing your car to coast to a halt. Be patient. Usually your arrival will disturb the animals but they will soon settle

IF YOU BREAK DOWN

Do not leave your vehicle. If you are within cellphone coverage, phone the nearest camp or gate. If you have no signal, flag down a passing motorist and give them a written note for the camp or gate stating clearly the road you are on – give the road number – and approximately where. If your vehicle develops a 'non-critical' mechanical problem seek advice at reception on the best course of action. Occasionally there's someone in camp who'd be able to help, failing which Vuswa Fleet Services is on call on toll-free 0800-03-0666.

Looking out over Pioneer Dam from the ladies bar in Mopani Camp.

Top: Ironically, in attempting to get a better view these folk are breaking the silhouette of their vehicle and spooking the animal.
Above: White-backed vulture.

down if you sit quietly. If you arrive and shout, move about your car noisily, dig into a loud plastic bag, your sighting is usually going to head for cover. Be particularly careful of electric windows. These are loud and certain animals are spooked by the noise; mechanical winders are best.

Certain animals, such as buffalo, will move off as you arrive, but will slowly return, sniffing the air cautiously, if you just sit patiently. Give them a chance to come back before you decide the sighting is over. Usually you can tell by the animal's body language whether it is disturbed by your presence. The big cats, for instance, will flick their tails like a domestic cat if they are feeling annoyed. The more vigorous the flick, the more likely they are going to leave.

Under no circumstances get out of your car to get a better look. Firstly, and probably more importantly, it is down-right dangerous. Animals in the park feel severely threatened by humans and if you get out of your car they can attack ... choosing fight over flight. Secondly, you teach the animals to associate humans, something they despise, with cars, something they care little about. If the association between cars and humans strengthens, animals will begin to avoid cars. Lastly, it's illegal and carries a heavy fine.

Game drives with kids

If you are travelling with young kids remember their attention span for wildlife may be significantly less than

GREAT BOOKS FOR KIDS

◆ *Ntini's Kruger Activity Book*, Jacana.

◆ *When Bat was a Bird and Other Tales from Africa*; *When Hippo was Hairy...*; *When Lion could Fly...*; and *When Elephant was King...* by Nick Greaves; Struik.

◆ *A South African Night* by Rachel Isadora; W Morrow Publishers.

◆ *A Young Explorer's Guide to the Bushveld* by Nadine Clarke; Struik.

◆ *The Adventures of Mick the Monk in the Kruger National Park*; *Mick the Monk in the Wild* and *Mick the Monk and the Birds of South Africa* by Ginger Gray; The Portfolio Collection.

yours. It helps to have 'activity packs' with which to occupy them when they become bored ... games, books and so on are great, but you will rue the day you allow the computer games! In addition, make the most of each sighting. In my experience, kids are fascinated with baboons and monkeys and will happily watch their antics way after adults have become bored.

Always take enough picnic goodies to allow you to stop at all the picnic sites where you can get out of the car, have a snack and a drink and allow the kids to let off some steam. Regular breaks are essential in counteracting the inevitable boredom that sets in.

Many camps teem with wildlife at night: bushbabies can often be seen and heard at most camps; Letaba is famous for its resident bushbuck; Satara and Shingwedsi for resident scops owlet; and genets often visit the units at Berg-en-Dal and Mopani. Insects such as praying mantis and stick insect can also provide fascinating viewing.

Another sure-fire way to keep the kids enthralled is to buy one of the great kids' books that are available and take every

GETAWAY'S SMARTIES™ GAME FOR EAGLE-EYED KIDS

First to spot this mammal ...	or this bird ...	or this tree ...	wins these Smarties
Dung beetle	Natal spurfowl	Mopane	One green
Slender mongoose	Fork-tailed drongo	Jackalberry	One red and brown
Duiker	White-backed vulture	Silver cluster leaf	One brown, pink and blue
Steenbok	Bateleur	Russet bushwillow	One purple and yellow
Buffalo	Double-banded sandgrouse	Weeping boerbean	One yellow, blue and green
Elephant	Ostrich	Sycamore fig	One purple, pink and red
Hippo	Tawny eagle	Rock fig	One brown
Rhino	Three-banded plover	Natal mahogany	One blue, yellow, brown and pink
Lion	Laughing dove	Baobab	One yellow, brown and green
Leopard	Paradise flycatcher	Leadwood	One blue, yellow, pink and purple
Cheetah	Malachite kingfisher	Fever tree	One purple, blue, pink, yellow and brown
Wild dog	Saddle-billed stork	Magic guarri	One blue, yellow, green, red, brown, pink and purple

THE BIG FIVE, 'LITTLE FIVE' AND BIRDING 'BIG SIX'

Big game hunters coined the term Big Five – lion, leopard, elephant, buffalo and rhino – in the mid-1800s to describe the most dangerous species they encountered on their hunts. It was believed that members of the Big Five were responsible for more deaths than all other species baring the mosquito.

Advertisers and marketers, who promote the idea of Big Five at every opportunity, have since hijacked the term and these days tourists flock to see the Big Five. Ironically, these species are now no longer a significant threat in Africa. Hippos and crocs kill more people annually than any other large mammal, while illnesses such as malaria (transmitted by the anopheles mosquito) are responsible for many thousands of deaths each year.

Recently, in order to combat the focus on Big Five, certain operators have coined two new terms: the 'little five' and 'birding big six'. The 'little five' – leopard tortoise, buffalo weaver, elephant shrew, ant-lion and rhino beetle – may be diminutive in size but are all fascinating creatures.

The 'birding big six' – martial eagle, kori bustard, ground hornbill, Pel's fishing owl, lappet-faced vulture and saddle-billed stork – are as majestic as any of the 'blue chip' species of the Big Five.

Don't forget to pack a soccer/rugby ball or a cricket bat and ball for the kids to knock around the camp in the evening. In fact why not join in yourself, but watch your hamstrings ... the nearest physio is in Nelspruit, I discovered.

Don't ignore other creatures in an obsession to tick off the Big Five – lion, leopard, elephant, buffalo and rhino.

opportunity to read excerpts when you come across the animals in question in the wild. Some of the larger camps have children's holiday programmes during SA school holidays – ask at reception. You should also take along a book for bedtime reading, as this is a perfect opportunity for some family bonding – especially if you are in one of the smaller accommodation units. My suggestion would be *Jock of the Bushveld*.

Where to stay

"The veld and animals of Nwanetzi are certainly not different to those of other camps, but whenever I get there, I have a strangely satisfying feeling that this particular veld and these animals are mine. Not quite 'my farm in the Bushveld', but still the haven for which I long whenever the tumult of the city gets a little too oppressive."

Piet Meiring, Kruger Park Saga

Kruger's accommodation is almost as diverse as its ecosystems and you can find something to fit just about any pocket, from inexpensive camp sites to ultra-luxurious private safari lodges. The south and central regions of the park boast numerous camps, accommodating the many visitors drawn by the remarkable numbers of predators and large herds of antelope that occur here. The northern region tends to be quieter as there are generally fewer animals and, consequently, fewer visitors, but camps such as Punda Maria nevertheless have their own special character and suite of attractions.

The following pages will help you choose a camp (divided into south, page 32; central, page 72; and north, page 114). Details are given on the accommodation available, animals to be seen and the best drives in the surroundings. Private concessions are dealt with on pages 138–155.

Enjoy your stay.

MY TOP FIVE SANPARKS CAMPS

◆ **Lower Sabie** for its wildlife – birds, predators, antelope ... you name it.
◆ **Satara** for the incredible density of predators in the area.
◆ **Bateleur** because it's out of the way, friendly and quiet.
◆ **Biyamiti**, as there's no better place to spot black rhino.
◆ **Punda Maria** and its surroundings have some of the best birding in the country, not to mention the fantastic archaeological sites.

The Southern Region

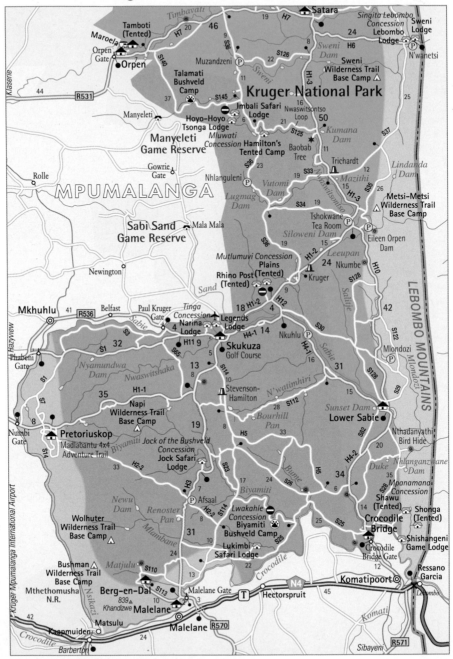

Crocodile Bridge
Southern Region

4

Formerly the headquarters of the old Sabi Reserve and one of Kruger's first four ranger posts, Crocodile Bridge is now a small gate camp 10 kilometres from Komatipoort. The camp is situated on the bank of the Crocodile River overlooking the old railway bridge – from whence it gets its name. This historic bridge was severely damaged during the devastating floods in 2000.

Although the camp overlooks the river, the far bank is outside the reserve and the farming activities may distract from any feeling of wilderness. As a transit camp, however, it takes some beating and its peaceful nature and plentiful wild-life nearby means you can squeeze in one last morning of game-viewing before heading home. When the ever-popular Lower Sabie camp is full, Crocodile Bridge makes a comfortable alternative.

Crocodile Bridge is a small camp on the Crocodile River.
White rhino (top) are common near the camp.

Accommodation

Chalets: Small three-bed units all with fridge/freezer and fully equipped kitchenette form a circle around a large grassy core dotted with false marula and other large trees.

Safari tents: Two-bed units are equipped with a fridge/freezer, but make use of communal kitchen and bathroom facilities.

Camping and caravanning: A relatively small, but pleasant caravan-and-camping site is located in the middle of the camp. Sites are not allocated. There is a small communal kitchen with two-plate hobs, as well as washing facilities and instant hot-water dispensers.

Some of Crocodile Bridge's safari tents are located next to the camp fence.

Wildlife

The camp: Scavenging baboons and vervet monkeys are regular visitors, so keep an eye on your food. Spotted hyenas also prowl the fence at night.

The surroundings: The Crocodile River area is densely populated with game because of its sweet grass plains dotted with marula trees and knobthorn acacias. These attract a variety of both grazers and browsers, which are inevitably followed by an entourage of predators. It is also good country for cheetah, which use the open plains to their advantage (particularly along the S28 and S137). Wild dogs are commonly seen, as well as rarer buck species such as reedbuck and nyala.

The Big Five: Both black and white rhino are common, while elephant and lion are regularly seen along the S25 west (Crocodile River Road). This is one of the best areas in the Kruger to see elephant herds. Buffalo can be difficult to find and you may need to head a little further north to see them.

Birds: The camp gardens have many flowering aloes in winter, which attract a host of sunbirds, starlings, weavers and bulbuls. Some of the park's rarer birds can be seen in the Crocodile Bridge area: keep a look out for purple-banded sunbird, yellow-rumped tinkerbird and black-bellied starling (which only occur in the very south of the park).

Don't miss!

The **Hippo Pool** (follow the S25 and then the S27 detour south) is a highlight. An armed ranger takes you to the water's edge about 3 km further, allowing you close-up sightings of hippos wallowing in a small pool on the Crocodile River. But do not get out of your car if not accompanied by a guard. Goliath heron, green-backed heron and little egret fish along the water's edge and, if you are lucky, you may see African finfoot. Orange-breasted

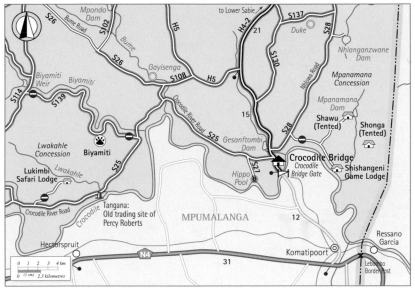

bushshrike, white-browed (Heuglin's) robin-chat and African (blue-billed) firefinch frequent the riverine bush.

There used to be rock art on a nearby overhang, but it was unfortunately obliterated in the 2000 floods.

Activities

Morning and sunset/night drives may be booked at reception.

Best drives

A number of good routes radiate from Crocodile Bridge and even though this small camp is on the very southern border of the park, the game-viewing is generally outstanding.

Crocodile River Road To reach the Crocodile River Road take the S25 about 2 km out of camp, which passes through mixed thornveld as it loosely tracks the course of the Crocodile River (the

short S27 detour south takes you to the hippo pool). The road continues along through attractive countryside offering fantastic game-viewing as wildlife congregates along the Crocodile River. It is worth driving the full length of the road to its intersection with the S114, where it is best to turn and retrace your steps. Elephant are all but guaranteed along this route, while white rhino, lion, giraffe, waterbuck, kudu and hyena are

Crocodile Bridge Gate is sometimes closed during periods of high rainfall.

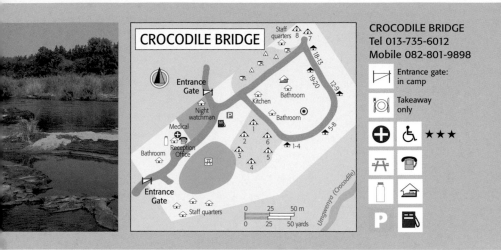

CROCODILE BRIDGE

Staff quarters 8 7
18-13
19-20
12-9

Entrance Gate

Kitchen
Bathroom
Night watchman
Bathroom
Medical
Reception Office
Bathroom
Staff quarters

1
2   6
3   5
4

5-8
1-4

Umgwenya (Crocodile)

0   25   50 m
0   25   50 yards

CROCODILE BRIDGE
Tel 013-735-6012
Mobile 082-801-9898

Entrance gate:
in camp

Takeaway
only

★★★

P

common. Look out for wild dogs as these are often seen in the early morning.

Nthandanyathi Loop This comprises the semicircular route created by the S130, S137 and S28. From the camp, take the H4-2 north towards Lower Sabie. The road passes through good game-viewing territory and offers good opportunities to see white rhino, wildebeest, zebra, giraffe and large concentrations of impala. Lion and leopard are also seen regularly here, while it is also renowned as a prime spot for wild dog. It is worth following the H4-2 all the way north to the S130 turn-off and then heading past **Duke Water Hole** on the S137, which often attracts interesting game including cheetah. Return via the **Nthandanyathi Bird Hide** and the road to **Nhlanganzwane Dam** (S28

Be sure not to miss Hippo Pool near Crocodile Bridge camp.

Wild dogs can often be seen near camp early in the morning or late in the evening.

Nhlowa Road) is prime white rhino territory (although the dam became poisoned and is closed).

The H5 (**Randspruit Road**), also off the H4-2, is not a particularly busy area of the park and yet it offers surprisingly good sightings. Hot spots in the area include the **Mpondo Dam** (on the S102 turn-off south), which often attracts a large amount of game and water birds. It is not really worth heading much further than the S102, and it may in fact be a good idea if you venture back along the attractive S26 (Bume Road). Another area worth investigating is the **Gayisenga Water Hole**, which often returns interesting sightings and is regularly visited by lions. On the road north towards Lower Sabie, culverts are sometimes used as hyena dens and you may even see young pups playing at the side of the road.

5 Biyamiti Bush Camp

Southern Region

Situated on the banks of the Biyamiti River, this bushveld camp boasts a fabulous setting and all 15 of the spacious units look out onto the attractive, sandy river course. A large shady lawn — courtesy of large jackalberries, among others — separates your cottage from the camp fence. The cottages are very private, making this an ideal getaway from the overcrowded feeling of some of the other camps. Game in the area is prolific and good sightings are almost guaranteed along the attractive private road leading into camp and the greater road network beyond.

Helmeted guineafowl (above) are common throughout the park and will often wander round the cottages in the quieter bushveld camps, such as Biyamiti (left).

Accommodation

Chalets There are five standard cottages with one bedroom, with two single beds, and a lounge with two sleeper couches; and 10 guest cottages with five beds in two bedrooms. All are fully equipped with two-burner stoves, fridge/freezers, crockery and cutlery.

Wildlife

The camp It is worth spending some time in the hide overlooking the river. Look for yellow-throated longclaw and red-faced cisticola in the long grass in front of the camp and nesting swallows in the eaves. At night civets, genets and galagos (bushbabies) are common.

The surroundings Look out for black rhino, although you are unlikely to see them from a vehicle. White rhino are plentiful, however. The area is also particularly good for leopard and wild dog. General game is abundant and waterbuck, duiker, steenbok, kudu and giraffe are regular sightings, but zebra and wildebeest are not common.

The Big Five You will almost certainly see rhino, and both elephant and leopard are common. Lion may be spotted on longer drives further north, while buffalo can be difficult to find.

Birds Biyamiti is a great place for bush birds: orange-breasted and grey-headed bush-shrike, black-crowned tchagra, striped and diderick cuckoo, green (red-billed) woodhoopoe, white-browed (Heuglin's) robin-chat, black-backed puffback, red-backed shrike, purple roller and scarlet-chested sunbird. In summer, you will be able to tick off woodland kingfisher and violet-backed (plum-coloured) starling. At night, listen out and look for African scops and barred owls and fiery-necked nightjar.

Don't miss!

The SANParks guided bushwalks are exciting and game, including white rhino (or – if you are very lucky – black rhino) are regularly seen at close quarters. Unlike the larger camps, however, refreshments are not provided and you need to take your own.

Activities

The morning and sunset drives are in a 12-seat vehicle, and are therefore slightly more costly than in the larger camps. Morning walks do not include snacks as is customary in the larger camps.

Best drives

(See route maps on page 32.) Because the camp is on a private road renowned for sightings of leopard, lion, wild dog, white rhino, elephant and kudu, you don't need to travel far to see game. Many visitors simply patrol the road, enjoying their sightings without hordes of other cars.

Biyamiti Loop Head north along the S139, crossing the **Biyamiti Weir**, keeping an eye

A lilac-breasted roller, probably the most visible bird in the park.

Above: Black rhino can be seen in the Biyamiti area if you are very lucky.
Below: Fever trees are often found lining the banks of streams and rivers.

out for interesting bird and animal life on the open plains. Zebra herds make this a favourite lion area and these large cats make regular kills. A small herd of sable also hangs out around here. On the far side of the river, take the S23 (**Biyamiti Loop**), following the course of the Biyamiti River before returning to the S114 and continuing on north.

Sightings generally improve as you approach **Renosterkoppies Dam** as game congregates in the area to drink. Possibly the highest concentration of rhinos in the park occurs here. It's worth driving past the **Stevenson-Hamilton Memorial Tablets** – take the S22 or S112, turning up to the **Shirimantanga Koppie** where a plaque commemorates the great man and his wife, whose ashes are scattered here. From here there are panoramic views of the southern part of the park.

Randspruit Road Loop This route

does not see many visitors, but often offers fantastic sightings. It is accessed by heading east from camp to the S25 (Crocodile River Road), and then north on the S26 (Bume Road).

Good sightings are often reported from **Mpondo Dam** on the S102, which crosses to the Randspruit Road. From this intersection, you can complete the loop in either direction as both offer good game-viewing, but the proximity of the Crocodile River Road to the river usually means this offers better sightings late in the day when animals are heading down to drink. Elephant are always seen along this route, while general game is exceptionally good,

> Your best chance of seeing black rhino is on a guided bushwalk in the southern regions of the park.

and lion, leopard and wild dog are all seen relatively often.

Crocodile River Road The only slight detraction from the otherwise excellent Crocodile River Road along the park's southern boundary is the proximity of the agricultural land on the far bank. Large numbers of elephant head down to the river in the afternoon to drink, while lion, leopard, wild dog and white rhino are fairly common. This route may be accessed either by heading east or west along the S139, but if you head west it is worth exploring the S118 (off the S114), past **James** and **Ampie se Boorgat water holes**, and the **Timfeneni Loop** before returning along the S114 and linking onto the Crocodile River Road. One advantage of this direction is that in the afternoon the sun does not set in your eyes, making game-viewing easier.

Too close for comfort: an impala herd reacts to a sound in the underbrush.

6
Malelane
Southern Region

Malelane is a small satellite camp near the Malelane Gate in the southwest of the park. The reception is at the gate, so make sure you arrive with enough time to complete formalities there and drive the 10-plus minutes to the camp.

Malelane is – much the same as Crocodile Bridge – an ideal 'transit' camp on your way into or out of the park.

Accommodation

Chalets Five old-style rondavels, with communal facilities and accommodating three or four people each, look south over the Crocodile River and, unfortunately, the agricultural land on the far side. A shady lawn surrounds the rondavels.

Camping and caravanning The sites are to the north and east of the camp. The area is grassy and has numerous electric points for caravan hook-ups – you need a caravan-plug adapter in order to use normal three-pin plugs.

Wildlife

The camp Baboons, monkeys and birds abound in the camp, while a number of tree species are represented. Look out for knobthorn acacias and sausage trees.

The surroundings The camp's immediate surroundings are not densely populated with wildlife so you need to drive north a short way in order to get into really good game areas. That said, leopard are often seen on the tar road leading to the gate, and in the opposite direction towards Berg-en-Dal camp, so you never know.... The best areas for game are along the Crocodile River – if you can ignore the unsightly human habitation on the far side of the river, outside the park. The entire area is good for white rhino.

The Big Five All five are regularly seen once you are in the more densely

Dwarf mongoose (top) often inhabit old termite mounds, while vervet monkey (above) regularly visit camp.

Leopard occur near Malelane camp; you are also sure to see giraffe in the area.

sunbirds attracted by the honeysuckle hedges; paradise flycatcher nest in the thorn trees. Lesser moorhen have been spotted near camp in summer, while half-collared kingfisher have been recorded on the bridge over the Crocodile River near Malelane Gate. The southern section of Kruger offers birders the opportunity to tick some of the larger raptors: martial eagle, tawny eagle, bateleur, African hawk eagle, and black-chested and brown snake eagle, as well as scavengers like white-backed vulture and marabou stork.

Don't miss!

Malelane camp can be unremarkable, but if you are staying at Malelane, it's likely you are on your way into or out of the park. Whether it's the first moment of calm or your last breath before diving into work once more, take time and smell the flowers.

frequented areas. The presence of large predators also guarantees a substantial hyena population.

Birds Crested barbet and cardinal woodpecker are often seen in the large trees in camp, while in summer the camp bustles with various

MALELANE

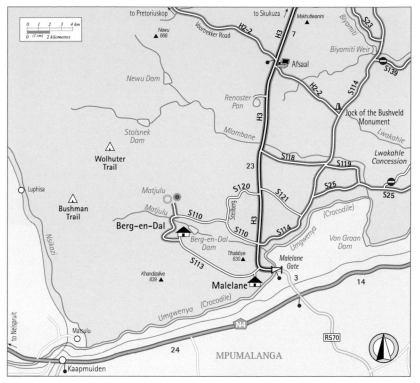

Activities

Guided game drives and night drives are offered from the Malelane Gate.

Best drives

Malelane shares the same conditions as Berg-en-Dal – visitors to this small camp often need to drive quite far for good sightings. That said, leopard are often spotted along the tarred S110 less than 1 km from the gate, and elephant, giraffe and small herds of other game, such as zebra and impala, are often seen en route to Berg-en-Dal. Otherwise, the route options are the same as those described under Berg-en-Dal.

Malelane has a pleasant, grassy camping area, with electrical points for caravans.

7 Berg-en-Dal

Southern Region

Often referred to as 'the rhino camp', this large, modern camp, situated in a botanical reserve and among the beautiful granite koppies in the southwest of the park, is the ideal base from which to launch your search for white rhino. Black rhino are also present in sizeable numbers, but they are notoriously shy of vehicles and you will be lucky to see them (although they are sometimes encountered on the guided walks from the camp).

If you are a park traditionalist, you will need to come to terms with the face-brick cottages. However, the peaceful, shady surroundings, modern restaurant and shop complex and child-friendly atmosphere make this a winner for visitors with children. There is room to explore, a fantastic swimming pool and an environmental-education unit that offers exciting activities during school holidays.

Known as 'the rhino camp' for the abundance of white rhinos (top) in the area, Berg-en-Dal's face-brick architecture (above) is a marked depature from traditional Kruger.

Accommodation

Chalets Berg-en-Dal's 69 chalets differ from traditional park rondavels and are square face-brick 'houses', complete with paved braai areas. The standard three-bed bungalows all have three fixed single beds, a small, fully equipped kitchenette and bathroom with shower.

The 23 family cottages sleep six (one bedroom has a double bed, another two singles and there are two sleeper couches in the lounge). All have showers and baths, and a fully equipped kitchenette. Two of the cottages are geared towards handicapped users and can be booked through central reservations.

Two guesthouses are also available. Rhino has four bedrooms, two with double beds and two with single beds. Le Roux has one with a double bed and two with single beds. The conference centre makes this camp a popular function and corporate venue.

Camping and caravanning The 70 sites are now allocated and visitors are allocated sites in the three large, shady camping areas. These are not grassed so bring along a groundsheet to help keep the dirt at bay. It is a good idea to arrive as early in the day as possible to claim your spot, especially if you want to camp on the fence line.

There are electric points (you will need a caravanning adapter to convert to standard three-pin plugs) distributed throughout the three areas and all have the standard parks communal kitchen units complete with two burner stoves, washing-up sinks and electric points. There are no communal freezers in the camp site.

BAT BOXES

Park authorities have battled for years with bats living in the accommodation units. These have unsettled many visitors and contribute to the rapid destruction of the thatch. The park has therefore launched a project to entice bats into custom-built 'bat boxes'. These small wooden boxes on tall stilts have so far proved a hit with the bats, so the bat problem is declining, allowing visitors and bats to co-exist peaceably.

Wildlife

The camp The dam near reception is home to hippo and crocodile, which are easily seen from the viewing area. You can sit and wait for the passing show – elephant, bushbuck and waterbuck are also often seen drinking at the dam, typically in the afternoons. Tall trees, including a quinine tree, provide shade, and lizards abound, including attractive blue-headed tree agamas.

The surroundings The area is excellent for rhino, and you are almost guaranteed to see them on drives and guided bushwalks. Berg-en-Dal is the only camp set amid rocky, hilly scenery. Leopards are commonly encountered near the camp and a resident leopard is known to visit the camp and patrol

Berg-en-Dal's takeaway restaurant offers visitors a range of inexpensive meals.

inside the fence. This is also a good area to see klipspringers (on the koppies), mountain reedbuck and grey rhebuck. Kudu, giraffe and warthog are common.

The Big Five Rhino are virtually guaranteed and you are very likely to see leopard too. Elephant are common, while lion may be seen on longer drives. Buffalo, however, can be difficult to spot. There is a good kudu population around the koppies.

Birds A resident fish eagle regularly swoops on unsuspecting fish in the dam adjacent to the camp. Sunbirds flit among the aloes and brown-headed parrots visit coral trees when they are in flower. Look out for white-browed (Heuglin's) and white-throated robin-chats, grey tit (fantailed) flycatchers and croaking cisticolas.

Don't miss!

The **Rhino Trail**, which ambles along the perimeter fence, is a great way to stretch your legs and, if you're lucky, spot game close to camp. It includes a short **Braille Trail** with plates in a few locations. Some trees are labelled. Only the first section of the trail is suitable for wheelchairs.

Activities

Morning and sunset drives are offered in either a large 20-seat or a smaller 12-seat vehicle; the smaller vehicle being slightly more exclusive and thus more expensive.

The morning and afternoon guided bushwalks (refreshments provided) are highly recommended, as you are likely to see, smell and hear rhino up close, a truly exhilarating experience. This, combined with the attractive scenery – granite koppies, tamboti thickets and so on – make this one of the best walking areas of the park.

Children are welcome in camp and there is a jungle gym near reception to keep them occupied. During school holidays a kiddies' programme run by the park's 'interpretive' staff allows par-

VAMPIRES OF THE VELD...

Redbilled oxpeckers – or tick birds, as they are sometimes called – pick ticks and earwax off a wide range of animals, including giraffe. Initially this relationship was thought to be purely mutualistic – in other words, both parties benefit by the interaction – but new research suggests that oxpeckers may be taking a slightly bigger slice of the pie. Evidence has shown that they do not significantly reduce parasite loads on their hosts, and worse, they seem to prolong the healing of sores on the animal. It appears that, in reality, these birds feed predominantly on blood from their hosts and dead tissue surrounding sores.

ents a few quiet moments if required.

On offer are bush braais away from the confines of the camp, allowing you to experience the romance of an open fire in the wilderness. These usually include a two-hour game drive. Wildlife

There is no better way to spend the heat of the day than in the camp pool.

documentaries are screened in a small open-air amphitheatre near reception every evening, weather permitting.

Best drives

Game-viewing in the immediate vicinity can be a little slow and in order to access good game routes you will need to head north along the H3 (Malelane–Skukuza Road) or east along the Crocodile River. The camp is, however, in a lovely setting, surrounded by picturesque granite koppies that are home to one of the most diverse floral assemblages in the park.

Matjulu Loop This route (along the S110) is a short drive from camp and passes through attractive scenery. Elephant and white rhino are relatively common and game, such as zebra, giraffe and impala, congregate around the **Matjulu Water Hole**. From here, retrace your steps and continue along the S110, taking the S120 turn-off,

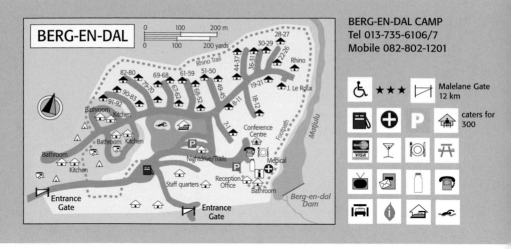

BERG-EN-DAL

0 100 200 m
0 100 200 yards

Rhino Trail

28-27
30-29
22-26
44-37
36-31
19-21
18-12
8-11
7-1

82-80
69-68
61-59
51-50
79-70
67-60
49-45
68-52
91-92
90-83

Rhino

J. Le Roux

Bathroom
Kitchen

Bathroom Kitchen

Bathroom

Kitchen

Staff quarters

Nightdrive/Trails

Conference
Centre

Footpath

Medical

Reception
Office

Bathroom

Matjulu

Berg-en-dal
Dam

**Entrance
Gate**

**Entrance
Gate**

BERG-EN-DAL CAMP
Tel 013-735-6106/7
Mobile 082-802-1201

★ ★ ★

Malelane Gate
12 km

caters for
300

which climbs steadily into mountainous terrain (no caravans are allowed on this road) covered with knobthorns, bushwillows, rock figs, white kirkia and others before topping out at a fantastic viewpoint overlooking the Malelane mountains. From here, the road descends sharply, eventually intersecting with the tarred H3 (Malelane–Skukuza Road).

Crocodile River Road This fantastic route follows the course of the Crocodile River east, and offers all sorts of exciting sightings. Elephant are almost guaranteed as they come down to the river to drink, while white rhino, lion, leopard, wild dog and large concentrations of general game are to be found. This route is productive at any time of the day and season.

As you head north on the H3 (Malelane–Skukuza Road), it is worth criss-crossing between this and the S25 and S114, along the S121 (**Timfeneni Loop**) and S118 past **James and Ampie se Boorgat water holes**. This

area is renowned for good sightings, with lion, white rhino, elephant and leopard often appearing alongside a variety of other game. When you reach **Afsaal**, a fully serviced picnic site at the juncture of the H3 and H2-2 (Voortrekker Road) with gas for hire, toilets, tables and chairs and a small shop and takeaway, you can either return the way you came or along the eastern stretch of the H2-2 and S114. The H2-2 follows the route transport riders used in the late 1800s as they moved goods between Delagoa Bay (the port of what is now Maputo) and the interior; Jock 'cairns' mark the way.

Once you hit the S114, it is worth exploring the southern turn-off to the productive **Mpambane Loop** (comprising the S119 and the S25), stopping at the **Gardenia Hide**, which overlooks a small water hole offering good sightings of general game and is a favourite warthog wallow. It is also good for flycatchers, which hawk insects from perches overlooking the water.

Pretoriuskop
Southern Region

Pretoriuskop is one of the oldest camps in the park and was the first to offer visitor accommodation, in the late 1920s, in the then Sabi Reserve. These days, some visitors prefer the busier camps further east, which tend to offer better game viewing, but I still love the 'old Kruger' feel of this camp. Moreover, it has huge amounts of space for kids, the best and first-built pool in Kruger – sculptured, in part, out of natural rock – and a revamped buffet restaurant, which would fit easily into a private lodge. A takeaway and well-stocked shop make this quiet camp a comfortable base for a couple of days.

Left: Pretoriuskop offers a wide range of accommodation. Above: One of the Jock cairns, which mark the historic Voortrekker route near camp.

Accommodation

Chalets There is a wide range of accommodation available. The most basic are school huts, which have two single beds and make use of communal kitchen and bathroom facilities. The 52 budget huts have two, three, five or six beds each. These are equipped with air conditioning and a small fridge/freezer, but kitchens and bathrooms are communal. The 54 bungalows have bathrooms, fridge/freezer and air conditioning;

> The massive, spreading Natal mahogany near the swimming pool is called 'the indaba tree' and is where Harry Wolhuter, the original ranger of the camp, used to hold staff meetings or discuss business matters with the leaders of the local people. Today it is home to a host of birds and a family of tree squirrels.

Above: The famous Indaba Tree.
Left: Watch out for sable near Pretoriuskop.

some have communal kitchen facilities while others include fully equipped kitchenettes. The four family cottages, with either two or three bedrooms (one of which contains a double bed and the others single beds), are best suited for larger families. All the cottages have two bathrooms, a kitchen and a lounge with television.

Two guesthouses accommodate larger groups. The Pierre Joubert sleeps 16 people in eight beds and eight sleeper couches, and the Doherty Bryant sleeps nine in three units, each containing a double bed and one single bed.

Camping and caravanning The camp site is pleasant and relatively shady – but only if you arrive in time to grab one of the spots under a tree. There is a small communal kitchen, although it has no fridge/freezer. Electrical boxes are scattered throughout the site, but you will need a caravanning-plug converter in order to use standard three-pin wall plugs. Individual sites are not allocated, and cannot be booked in advance, so it's a matter of first come, first served.

Wildlife

In camp A small impala herd grazes the lawns surrounding the huts, carefully cropping away at the grass. Hyenas often patrol the fence.

The surroundings The immediate surroundings are good for game such as kudu and waterbuck. Sable, tsessebe, common reedbuck, eland and Lichtenstein's hartebeest are likely to be seen in the area, but they are not common. This is one of the few places in the park where the diminutive red

Pretoriuskop has the best swimming pool in all of Kruger.

duiker and oribi are also found.

The Big Five This is not a particularly good area for lion, although they are seen on occasion. Leopard, elephant, buffalo and rhino are regularly seen on drives from the camp.

Birds Keep an eye out for sunbirds, barbets and brown-headed parrots especially when the coral trees and aloes are in flower. Purple-crested turacos (louries) often visit in summer when there is fruit on the marula trees.

Don't miss!

A dip in the most attractive swimming pool in Kruger is a highlight, but also be sure to be on the lookout for the rare oribi, which you will see nowhere else in Kruger, and other antelope species. It is also well worth following the **Sable Trail** through camp. There is a small museum and info centre next to the Sable statue.

Activities

Guided early-morning, mid-morning, sunset and night drives are offered in

JOCK OF THE BUSHVELD

Jock is undoubtedly South Africa's most famous dog. He was the main character in Sir Percy Fitzpatrick's bestselling *Jock of the Bushveld* – based on his days as a young transport rider working the old route to Lourenço Marques (Maputo). The young man and his Staffordshire-cross terrier, Jock, became inseparable, and a number of important 'Jock sites' are now marked in the south of the park, indicating places where modern roads intersect with the old trading routes used by Fitzpatrick. In addition, a new lodge – Jock Safari Lodge – has been constructed on a private concession in the area (see page 150). The lodge is themed on Jock's story and everything, even the dog biscuits you get with your afternoon high tea, is in character.

Jock stayed with his owner until 1889, when Fitzpatrick lost his oxen to tsetse fly and his horses to nagana (African horse sickness). Ruined, he walked into Barberton then took up a job with the Corner House Mining Company in Johannesburg. Jock was given to a friend who ran a trading store in Pessene in Mozambique. One night, the now-deaf Jock was accidentally killed while apprehending a predator in the chicken coop. He had successfully chased off the intruding beast but was mistakenly identified as a jackal and shot by his new owner.

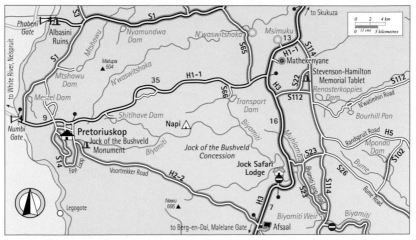

The Madlabantu Adventure Trail near camp accommodates 4x4 enthusiasts.

a 10- or 23-seat vehicle – the larger vehicle being less expensive. These are all booked at reception. The four-hour morning bushwalks (refreshments included) and three-hour afternoon bushwalks (refreshments included) can also be booked at reception, but a maximum of eight people are accepted on a walk.

Bush braais on one of the nearby koppies include a three-hour drive and there is a cash bar on site. The **4x4**

Madlabantu Adventure Trail (roughly 4^1/$_2$ hours, depending on your stops) leaves from Pretoriuskop. The southern stretch is frankly very tame and the only tricky sections are the two river crossings, which do not pose any difficulties in the dry season. The northern parts are more challenging, where slightly more skill in 4x4 driving is required; book at reception on the day of the trail. Advance bookings are not accepted. Wildlife documentaries are shown in the camp's small open-air theatre if weather permits.

Best drives

Pretoriuskop is situated in the Pretoriuskop Sourveld Ecozone, which is characterised by tall grass and thick bush that make game-viewing tricky in places. That said, many good routes are indeed accessible and offer a combination of fantastic scenery and good game viewing.

Fayi Loop The collection of dirt roads that make up the S14 (Fayi Loop) to the south of the camp pass through beautiful scenery encompassing granite koppies protruding from a sea of tall grass studded with mixed bushwillows, kiaat, knobthorn acacias and so on. The grass can make game viewing difficult, but kudu and baboon are common and white rhino, sable and leopard are all seen occasionally. This region includes some of the best landscape and views in the whole park – which makes up for the lack of wildlife.

Albasini Road The S3 (Albasini Road) is named after the trader João Albasini who was an important trader in the region, operating a chain of stores that supplied transport riders moving between Lydenburg and Delagoa Bay (Maputo). It heads north from the H1-1 near Numbi Gate, passing the **Mestel Dam**, which is usually surrounded by good game, mainly waterbuck and, in thicker vegetation, bushbuck, but because the entire route runs through sourveld, game-viewing may be difficult along the rest of the way. This improves after you cross the S1 (Doispane Road) where the vegetation changes to mixed thornveld, before reaching the Sabie River where it follows the course, passing through mixed thornveld interspersed with thick riverine vegetation characterised by tall sycamore figs, jackalberries, leadwoods and so on. Once you reach the river on the S3 (Sabie River Road), game viewing usually improves dramatically and this road can be very rewarding, with lion, elephant, leopard, rhino, kudu and a host of other species regularly seen. Also take time to watch for smaller animals such as dwarf mongoose, which

Look out for purple-crested turacos in camp.

otherwise you might miss. When you reach the S3 intersection with the S4, turn for home via the S1. Alternatively, take the S65 past the **Nwaswitshaka Water Hole**.

Napi Road The H1-1 (Napi Road) is an attractive road, offering views over southern Kruger and passing interesting watering spots and landscape features. Take the short detour to **Shitlhave Dam**. This is a magnet to game in the area and often attracts a collection of general wildlife and water birds, such as three-banded plover, black-winged stilt, blacksmith lapwing, black-crowned night heron and malachite kingfisher. The H1-1 passes both the **Napi Koppie** (505 m) and the turn-off to **Transport Dam**, another large dam well worth the short detour.

Further east along the Napi Road is the northerly turn-off of the S65,

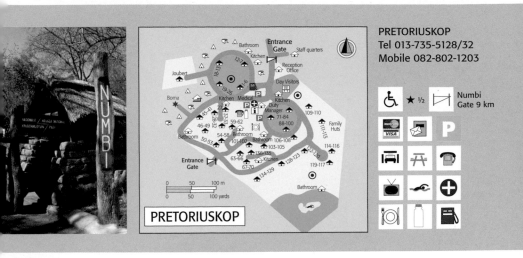

PRETORIUSKOP
Tel 013-735-5128/32
Mobile 082-802-1203

Numbi
Gate 9 km

PRETORIUSKOP

Guided morning and evening bushwalks are offered at Pretoriuskop.

which leads to the **Nwaswitshaka Water Hole,** a hot spot for game. Lion are regularly seen and the open grassy sweetveld hosts herds of zebra, wildebeest and other grazers. A family of ground hornbills is also regularly seen, so keep a lookout for these easily recognisable, black, turkey-sized birds.

From Nwaswitshaka continue north along the S65 to the Doispane Road and return that way, or retrace your steps and continue a little further along the H1-1 to visit the **Stevenson-Hamilton Memorial Tablets**, 10-plus kilometres after the intersection. If there is still time, head home past **Renosterkoppies Dam** (also called the **Shirimantanga Dam**) which is usually surrounded by large numbers of game. Rhino are regularly seen, while lion and leopard are reported frequently.

Voortrekker Road The H2-2 (Voortrekker Road) heads east, skirting the base of Ship Mountain, which was a popular camping spot for the transport riders in the late 1800s. A small plaque commemorates the birthplace of Percy Fitzpatrick's famous dog, Jock. The site itself is a short detour from the main road, with not much to recommend it apart from its historical significance. The entire Voortrekker Road is, however, often rewarding, with many lion, wild dog, leopard, white rhino, elephant and kudu sightings. It ends a short distance from the popular **Afsaal Picnic Site**, which is well serviced and has toilets, gas cookers for hire, chairs and tables, as well as a small shop and takeaway restaurant.

9 Lower Sabie
Southern Region

This is undoubtedly one of the most popular camps in the park — and with good reason. The wildlife here is prolific and it's an excellent spot to see the Big Five. In addition, it occupies a wonderful location on a bank of the Sabie River, a short distance upstream from a small weir that dams the river in front of camp. Magnificent old sycamore figs, coral trees, fever trees and jackalberries are dotted throughout, and birdlife abounds. There is plenty of space for the kids to unwind on the grassy lawns under the trees, while you enjoy sundowners in the snazzy, new restaurant and bar area overlooking the water. (Be warned, however, that mosquitos can be a problem in the evening, so it is best to wrap up in long pants and shirt.)

Lower Sabie is famous for its tall trees and soothing river views.

Accommodation

Due to its popularity, it is essential to book accommodation well in advance, as the camp tends to be full year-round.

Chalets The four one-bed huts are not equipped with kitchen utensils, cutlery and crockery, although the two-, three- and five-bed huts (26 in total) do have a fridge and basin. They all utilise communal ablutions and kitchens. The two-bed bungalows (not equipped) have a bathroom, and three-bed bungalows are equipped with both kitchenettes and bathrooms. Of the 60 units, 46 have a perimeter view and are consequently more costly.

The two, two-roomed family bungalows sleep a maximum of five all in single beds, two in one room and three in the other.

Steenbok and Moffat guesthouses each have two bedrooms and sleep four, while the Keartland Guesthouse sleeps seven people in three rooms. Each bedroom has its own bathroom with baths and showers. All the guesthouses are fully equipped, including proper stoves, while Keartland also boasts DStv.

A new boardwalk leads upstream from the restaurant along the Sabie River, offering excellent views and associated biodiversity.

Safari tents The 24 new safari tents sleep two and have a small en-suite bathroom. Of these, 12 have a river view.

Camping and caravanning There are 34 clearly demarcated gravel sites, each with its own braai spot and electric box requiring a caravanning adaptor for regular thee-pin plugs. Some sites are allocated, but there are precious few with any shade.

Young hippo bulls spar in the Sunset Dam. Below: a blue-eared glossy starling.

Wildlife

The camp The large sycamore figs, sausage trees, fever trees and jackalberries lining the Sabie River give the camp a shady, relaxed feel and attract a wide range of birdlife, especially as they bear fruit for much of the year. Elephant, hippo, buffalo and other game congregate at the water to drink and are easily viewed from camp.

The surroundings
The Lower Sabie area teems with life and you are sure to see a wide range of animals, from large crocodiles and hippos in the Sunset Dam to leopards along the river course. The entire area is also good for wild dog, which are sometimes seen early in the mornings along the roads radiating out from camp. Further south, cheetah are often

encountered. Warthogs occur in large numbers in the area.

The Big Five All members of the Big Five are present in good numbers in the area and, on lucky days, all may be seen on a single outing.

Birds The trees in camp attract numerous species, in particular hornbills, green pigeons, barbets and a host of other fruit-eating species. Sunbirds, weavers and starlings are also common in camp. At night, listen out for square-tailed (Mozambique) and fierynecked nightjars and the deep grunt of Verreaux's (giant) eagle owl. Sunset Dam is a good place for a range of water birds: African jacana, goliath heron and saddle-billed, woolly-necked, yellow-billed, openbilled and black stork. Hamerkop are always present and African spoonbill prowl the shallows, while malachite kingfisher flit overhead. White-crowned lapwing are also often seen here as well as near the N'watimhiri causeway on the road to Skukuza. White-fronted bee-eater occur in the dongas along the road to Skukuza a few kilometres from camp. On the grassy plains north of camp, look for ostrich, kori and black-bellied bustard, red-crested korhaan, Swainson's spurfowl, common and harlequin quail as well as kurrichane buttonquail.

Don't miss!

Watch the sun slip below the horizon at **Sunset Dam** as the guineafowls flock into the branches of the dead leadwoods for the night and young male hippos spar with each other in the water below.

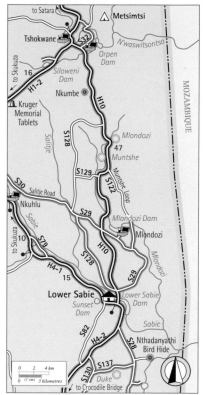

LOWER SABIE

Also be on the lookout for the area's wild dog, lion, leopard, elephant, rhino and giraffe.

Activities

Three-hour morning and sunset drives in 20-seat vehicles can be booked at reception. Guided, early-morning bush-walks, which include refreshments, provide you with an excellent chance of meeting white and black rhino, together with a host of other wildlife, on foot.

Bush braais are popular, so book well in advance. Wildlife documentaries are shown daily, weather permitting.

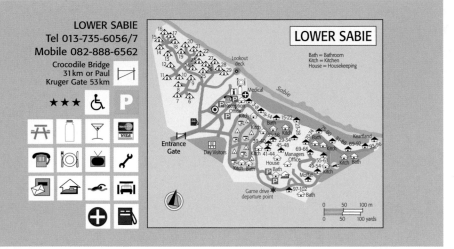

Best drives

Lower Sabie is surrounded by fantastic routes, all of which offer sightings on a regular basis. It lies in the bottom corner of the **Leopard Triangle**, comprising Skukuza, Nkuhlu Picnic Site and Lower Sabie. Here, where the Sabie and Sand rivers meet, you will find the most extensive stretch of riverine forest in the Lowveld. One of the best spots for game hardly requires a drive – **Sunset Dam** is less than a kilometre from the gate, and provides great crocodile, hippo and water bird sightings. It is also a favourite hunting spot for wild dog, which regularly attack herds of impala that gather to drink at sunset.

Skukuza-Lower Sabie Road The main 'drag', the H4-1 (Skukuza–Lower Sabie Road) along the Sabie River, is one of the busiest roads in the park ... and rightly so. Elephant, kudu, lion, leopard, wild dogs – you name it – are regularly seen along this route, and you could wrap up your game viewing in a morning on a good day.

It's worth heading all the way out to **Nkuhlu Picnic Site** (fulcrum of the Leopard Triangle) where there are gas cookers for hire, toilets, chairs and tables, a small shop and takeaway. The monkeys and starlings may be entertaining, but don't feed them! After this the road tends to get busier and busier and it is probably better to return home the way you came. Alternatively, if you can face the people, head up to the H12, which crosses the Sabie River (look out for great water bird sightings at the low bridge, as well as crocs and hippos) and return along the S30 (Salitje Road) and then the S128 or H10.

Muntshe Loop To take in the Muntshe Loop, head north from the camp on either the H10 or S29, passing **Mlondozi Dam Picnic Site**. Although this lofty view over the dam provides you with pretty scenery, it is unfortunately a little far for any great wildlife sightings, but look out for the resident mocking cliff-chats. Then, taking either the S122 or H10, circle the **Muntshe**

You may not realise it, but Lower Sabie Rest Camp is only 11 km from the Mozambican border.

Above: Look for chameleons on night drives. Top: Early evening from the low-water bridge near Lower Sabie.

Mountain (444 m), which is one of the prime spots in the park to see sable and mountain reedbuck. These routes pass through open grassy plains. Elephant, lion and large herds of buffalo are often seen here, particularly in the dry winter months. Exciting sightings are possible along the entire route and lion, leopard, elephant, hippo, bushbuck, white rhino, waterbuck and giraffe are all common.

Gomondwane Road The H4-2 (Gomondwane Road) heading south from Lower Sabie offers a huge number of exciting sightings, from elephant, white rhino and giraffe to wildebeest, zebra and lion, all of which are common, while leopard are seen regularly. Cheetah are often reported around **Duke Water Hole**, while wild dog are often reported closer to Crocodile Bridge. It is worth heading all the way south to Crocodile Bridge before returning along the S28 (Nhlowa Road) past **Nhlanganzwane Dam** and **Nthandanyathi Hide.**

Skukuza

Southern Region

10

Above: The clock tower near Skukuza's reception.
Right: The camp's architecture follows traditional lines and consists predominantly of thatched rondavels.

The administrative headquarters of the park and Kruger's largest rest camp, Skukuza positively buzzes with activity. Situated on the southern bank of the perennial Sabie River, in one of the best game-viewing areas of the park, it is popular year-round. The name Skukuza originates from Stevenson-Hamilton's Shangaan nickname, meaning 'turns everything upside down' or 'sweeps clean' after his efforts to turn the then Sabi Reserve, the forerunner of the Kruger National Park, into a viable conservation area.

Accommodation

Chalets The best units are those down-river from the shop and restaurant complex. The simplest of the chalets are two- and three-bed bungalows (117 units), which make use of communal kitchen facilities. The 61 two- and three-bed bungalows have basic kitchen facilities, while there are 15 two-person, luxury, riverside bungalows with magnificent views over the Sabie River. These are somewhat of a departure from traditional SANParks bungalows and have large plate-glass windows, fancy outside cooking and braai areas, double beds and satellite TV. In addition Skukuza boasts four-, six-, seven- and nine-bed guest cottages, all of which have a fully equipped kitchenette. Guesthouses for larger groups include Moni, Nyathi and Waterkant, which sleep eight each, and Absa, which sleeps 12 (four are accommodated in the lounge on sleeper couches).

Safari tents Two- and four-bed units are available, but all make use of communal kitchens and bathroom facilities. Each unit is equipped with a small fridge/freezer.

Camping and caravanning The large, 80-site camping area (some of the sites are numbered) is spread over a wide area to the east of the rest camp. There are braai facilities near most sites and electric boxes are well appointed throughout, although you will need a caravanning adapter for regular three-pin wall plugs.

Communal kitchens with washing sinks, two-plate electric stoves and instant boiling water dispensers and a laundromat are strategically placed throughout.

Wildlife

The camp Elephant, hippo, crocodile, giraffe, impala, waterbuck and other species can be seen coming down to the Sabie River to drink. A large number of bats usually roost under the thatched roof outside the takeaway restaurant. At night, bushbabies are sometimes seen leaping from tree to tree. Look out for the pair of whitetailed mongoose that live near the Papenfus Tower.

The surroundings This is one of the best game-viewing areas in the park. Wild dog are often seen along the surrounding roads early in the morning. Hyena are also very common around Skukuza and this is one of the best areas in the park to view these interesting and often-maligned predators. The entire river drainage area is crowded with life, and whether you drive around or find a good vantage point over the river – in which case look out for giant water monitors – you are likely to be richly rewarded.

The Big Five Lion are seen frequently in the area, while leopard are seen every day (according to the sightings board) along the densely vegetated river margins. Elephant are abundant in the Sabie River and large buffalo herds visit relatively often. Rhino can be slightly trickier to find but do occur in the area.

Birds A large number of bird species are attracted to the majestic trees that shade the camp – in particular, look out for the African green pigeon, brown-headed parrot and paradise, black, dusky, spotted, grey tit (fan-tailed) and pallid flycatcher. In summer, massive nesting colonies of lesser-masked and village (spotted-backed) weavers con-

gregate near the restaurant. Bat hawk and Eurasian hobby are often seen over the river, while African finfoot and half-collared kingfishers are not uncommon. Look for these birds at the low-level bridge over the Sabie.

The river walk can be very productive, with sightings of collared sunbird, red-backed and bronze mannikin, red-faced cisticola, spectacled weaver, purple-crested turaco, orange-breasted, grey-headed as well as gorgeous bushshrikes.

It is worth visiting the nearby hide at **Lake Panic**, which offers fantastic viewing of various water birds including black-winged stilts, kingfishers and herons – not to mention crocodiles and terrapins – at close quarters.

Above: View over the Sabie River from the restaurant. Top: A visit to the Stevenson-Hamilton Memorial Library is a must.

Don't miss!

The **Stevenson-Hamilton Memorial Library and Museum**, with its impressive collection of historical accounts and interesting displays, is not to be missed.

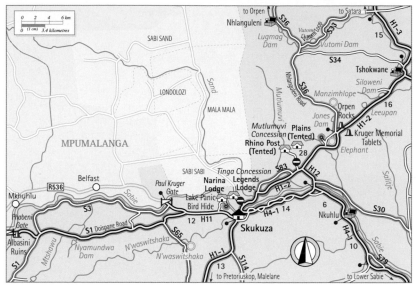

On display is the skin of the lion killed by Harry Wolhuter, and the sheath knife that delivered the death blow.

Drop in on the **Selati Grillhouse** (an old restored train). There is a 9-hole golf course (013-735-5543), indigenous plant nursery, wetland boardwalk, and a day visitor's centre including a swimming pool and braai lapa.

Activities

Guided early-morning, mid-morning, sunset and night drives are offered in a 10- or 23-seat vehicle – the larger ones being less expensive. These are all booked at reception. Four-hour morning bushwalks and three-hour 'sunset' bushwalks, with a maximum of eight people, can also be booked here. Bush braais including a three-hour drive and a cash bar on site are booked at the restaurant or at reception. Wildlife documentaries are shown, weather permitting, in the open-air auditorium.

Best drives

The problem with Skukuza is often not finding animals but avoiding the hordes of other visitors when you do. All the main roads in the vicinity are busy and you are unlikely to have many sightings to yourself, unless you wait for the 'hordes' to return to camp for breakfast; from 08h00 to 10h00 all but the most popular roads will be quiet. On the positive side, the frequency of cars has habituated many animals so good sightings are often possible. There are also a number of less busy routes around the camp and, on these, you often encounter animals without too many people.

Doispane Loop Heading west towards the **Paul Kruger Gate** on the S42 (Kruger Gate Road), pass the intersection with the S1 and continue on the H11 almost to the gate, taking the left turn onto the S3 river road. This hugs the banks of the Sabie River and passes through thick riverine vegetation. Exciting sightings beckon on the route and lion, leopard, elephant, hippos, bushbuck, white rhino, waterbuck and giraffe are common. Wild dog are also regularly spotted in the early morning. Keep to the S3 until it intersects with the S1 near the **Phabeni Gate**. At this point, it is worth heading west towards the gate for a short distance to see the **Albasini Ruins**, where the trader João Albasini had his house and trading store in the mid-1800s. There are toilets and a small info centre at the site. Then retrace your steps and continue east along the S1, known as the Doispane Road, after the legendary ranger Doispane Mongwe.

It is well worth visiting the **Nyamundwa Dam**, where impala, wildebeest, kudu and waterbuck often congregate to drink. Water birds such as black crake, moorhen, African spoonbill and hamerkop are also always present, as are hippo, terrapin and crocodile. Continue on the S1 to the S65, turning off to the **Nwaswitshaka Water Hole**. The road is very close to the water here, allowing fantastic views of game drinking. A family of ground hornbills patrols this area so keep an eye open for these endangered birds. General game such as zebra, impala, kudu and giraffe occur along the whole route and there is also a good chance of seeing lion.

Skukuza-Lower Sabie Road The H4-1, which heads east from Skukuza, is probably the busiest road in the park, carrying traffic from two large camps and a large number of day-trippers.

The open grassy plains north of Skukuza teem with species such as giraffe.

Skukuza is full of history, including attractions such as the Selati Railway (above right), which now functions as a restaurant.

However, its popularity is not without good reason and fantastic sightings are almost guaranteed. Elephant are very common along the entire course of the Sabie River, while a huge number of impala mill about near the road. Be sure to take the turn-offs from the H4-1, both towards and away from the river, as there are often sightings along these. Nearly all the pools in the river contain hippos, and large crocs sun themselves along the bank. Baboons and monkeys are also common along this road and you can spend hours watching their antics. In the evenings, keep a lookout for leopard, regularly seen by visitors returning to Skukuza at last light.

Midway between Skukuza and Lower Sabie is **Nkuhlu Picnic Site**, which boasts gas cookers for hire, toilets, chairs and tables, a takeaway and small shop selling a relatively wide range of essentials. You can turn back here or continue on to Lower Sabie as the entire route provides fantastic viewing. The Nkhulu Picnic Site is the epicentre of the 'leopard triangle'. Also heavy elephant traffic from the river crosses the road into the dense bush. Check all the short detour loops along the river for game sightings.

Tshokwane Road This is another popular route, accessed either by heading along the H4-1 a short distance and crossing the Sabie River on the H12, or by following the H1-2 from Skukuza, crossing the Sabie and Sand rivers. Whichever option you choose, keep a lookout from the low-level bridges as you cross the rivers as great views of hippo, giant water monitors, crocodile and water birds, like darter, reed and white-breasted cormorant, little bittern, green-backed, goliath and squacco heron are possible. Where the H1-2 crosses the Sand River is a hot

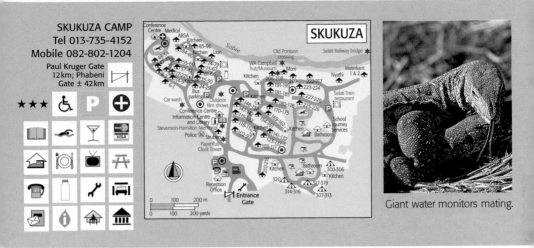

SKUKUZA CAMP
Tel 013-735-4152
Mobile 082-802-1204

Paul Kruger Gate
12km; Phabeni
Gate ± 42km

SKUKUZA

Giant water monitors mating.

spot for both lion and leopard. The H1-2 is also good for elephant and large herds are often seen grazing on the thornveld next to the road. Closer to the Sand River, large troops of baboon and vervet monkey frequent the jackalberries, sycamore figs and other majestic trees that line the banks of the Sand River. You can make this a short loop and return along the H12 to the H4-1 and home, but if you have the time, head north to **Tshokwane**.

The excellent H1-2, with its numerous dams and water holes, attracts a range of wildlife, and lion, leopard, buffalo and elephant sightings are common. Six kilometres north of the intersection with the H12 you have an option to turn left onto the S84, which takes you past the **Mantimahle Dam**, while if you stick with the tar road you pass **Olifants Water Hole**. Both the dam and the water hole offer great opportunities, although the S86 dirt road loop is a little less busy. Old-timers consider these the two best game-viewing dams in Kruger.

After you rejoin the H1-2, you pass the **Kruger Memorial Tablets** where you can stop, alight and walk up to the brass plaques for a close look. It's a good excuse to stretch your legs, but be aware as there is always the chance of spotting animals in the vicinity. Continuing along, it's worth visiting **Leeupan** water hole and **Silolweni dam** before reaching the **Tshokwane Picnic Site,** which includes a pub with draught beer on tap and boerewors rolls. The birds are particularly tame at Tshokwane so take your binoculars and bird books along, as fantastic sightings of hornbills, glossy starlings and a range of other species are possible.

Malelane–Skukuza Road Head south on the H1-1, the main road leading south to Malelane. A short distance along the S114, a dirt road branches off and you can take either road. If you stick with the tar, you avoid the dust and you pass the **De Laporte Water Hole** and impressive **Mathekenyane View Point**, from where you half

The Central Region

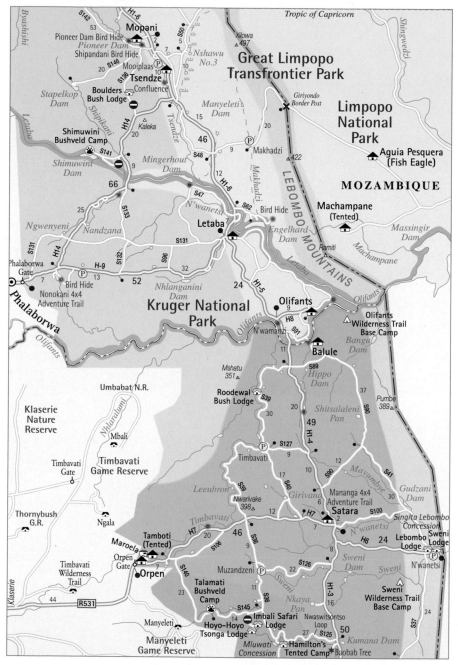

Orpen, Maroela and Tamboti

Central Region

11

Don't overlook the newly expanded Orpen Complex, which includes a day centre and swimming pool. There is plenty of game in the attractive thornveld that surrounds Orpen and its satellite camps, Maroela Caravan Camp and Tamboti Tented Camp, providing plenty of game-viewing opportunities. The camp is named in honour of the Orpen family, in particular Eileen Orpen, who donated a large portion of pristine bushveld to the park (see the plaque at the Rabelais Dam nearby).

Located at Orpen Gate, Orpen is a convenient transit camp for the park's central regions.

Accommodation

Chalets Orpen's two- and three-bed huts have bathrooms and communal kitchen facilities. There are also six-bed, fully equipped guest cottages available.
Safari tents At Tamboti Tented Camp, 3km from Orpen, the two- and four-bed units have fridge/freezers and braai places. All utilise communal ablutions and kitchen facilities.
Camping and caravanning At Maroela, just 2km from Orpen, all the sites are sandy and none are allocated. Shady spots are limited so get in early to claim your spot. Both Tamboti and Maroela are along the Timbarati River.

Wildlife

The camp Occasionally, jackal, porcupine and honey badger wander through the camp, which makes an exciting change from the regulation

There is no better place in the park to see cheetah than along the H7 between Satara and the Orpen Gate. Top: At Orpen Dam there's a viewpoint and picnic site.

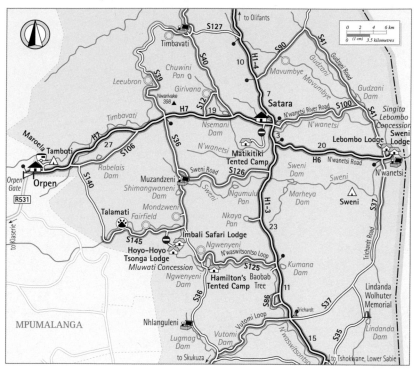

baboons and vervet monkeys. In the early evening, lesser galagos (bush-babies) can be seen leaping about as they head out into the night.

The surroundings The area is good for cheetah, which hunt on the open plains to the east of camp. Sable are common and a large pack of wild dog is frequently seen on drives from the camp. General game, including zebra, wildebeest and impala, is good on the gabbro-soil flats.

The Big Five Rhino can be difficult to find but try the **Rabelais Loop** around the **Rabelais Dam**. Herds of elephant are everywhere and lion are regularly seen on the open grassy plains around

the Maroela turn-off, some 3km from the gate. Buffalo are regulars, while leopard often occur in the immediate vicinity of the camp.

Birds White-backed vulture are often seen in the area, and large numbers may indicate a kill. In summer, look out for nesting paradise flycatcher in camp. Black-winged lapwing are common at the water hole near the camp gate.

Don't miss!

The open plains around the turn-off to Maroela and Tamboti provide one of the best chances of seeing a cheetah kill in the park. Orpen dam has a webcam (www.sanpark.org/webcams).

Activities

Book your morning and sunset drives and guided morning and afternoon bush walks at reception. Wildlife documentaries are shown in the open-air auditorium, weather permitting.

Best drives

You don't have to drive far from Orpen to see great sightings – lion, cheetah, sable and a host of other wildlife are often reported from the open grassy areas around the turn-off to Maroela, a couple of kilometres from camp. However, if you want to head further, there are a number of good routes for you to follow (see also 'Best drives' in Satara on page 80).

Talamati Loop Head east on the H7 (Satara Road), taking the S106 (Rabelais Road) turn past **Rabelais' Hut**. Immediately after the hut, turn right onto the S140 towards the Talamati Bushveld Camp. This heads south, passing through mixed grasslands dotted with bushwillow and knobthorn acacias before eventually turning east to follow the course of the Nwaswitsontso River. The first half of this route may be a little dull but after you get to the riverine vegetation along the Nwaswitsontso, things generally get more interesting. Here good lion sightings are common and leopard are regularly spotted along the river. Kudu, waterbuck, giraffe and elephant as well as a variety of other game are nearly always seen.

Continue past Talamati, dropping by **Fairfield** and **Mondzweni water holes**, both of which have a fantastic reputation for game-viewing. At the intersection of the S145 (Talamati Road) with the S36 (Nhlanguleni Road), head north and stop at the **Shimangwaneni Dam**, where large herds of elephant often drink. You can break your drive further north at the **Muzandzeni Picnic Site** (which has toilets, gas cookers, cold drinks, picnic areas and even washing facilities) before continuing up to the H7 and left, back to Orpen.

Satara Road Following the H7 east to Satara is an extremely reward-

Above Maroela Camp.
Left: Tamboti Camp.
Right: Crested barbet.

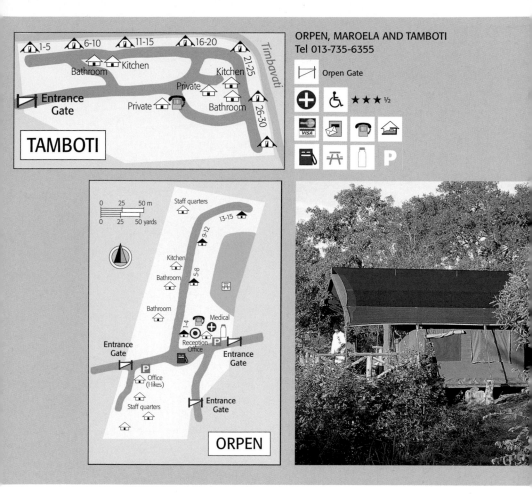

TAMBOTI

1-5 6-10 11-15 16-20

21-25

26-30

Bathroom Kitchen

Kitchen

Private

Private Bathroom

Entrance
Gate

Timbavati

ORPEN

0 25 50 m
0 25 50 yards

Staff quarters

13-15

9-12

Kitchen

5-8

Bathroom

Bathroom

Medical

1-4

Reception
Office

Entrance
Gate

Entrance
Gate

Office
(I-likes)

Entrance
Gate

Staff quarters

ing route, passing through open grassy areas frequented by herds of wildebeest and zebra. Giraffe, elephant and warthog are also frequently seen here. Take the right-hand turn-off to the S106, past **Rabelais' Hut** and stop off at the **Rabelais Dam**, which always produces good sightings, as large groups of elephant, giraffe, zebra and waterbuck often gather to drink. Shortly after the S106 rejoins the H7, take the turn-off to **Bobbejaan Krans** (baboon cliff). This site offers visitors panoramic views over the Talamati River, where crocodiles have been seen taking impala.

About 7km further north, past the intersection with the S36 (south) and the S39 (north), take the short S12 loop to the left, past the **Girivana Water Hole**. This little loop is often very busy, with buffalo, elephant, lion and leopard often recorded in the area. After this, you can return to Orpen or continue on to Satara for brunch.

12 Satara
Central Region

This is the second largest camp after Skukuza and is extremely popular, largely due to the prolific wildlife that wanders the surrounding plains. In particular, Satara is renowned for its lion sightings and you will not spend much time here without encountering at least one of these tawny favourites. The 'lion triangle', where visitors are more or less guaranteed lion sightings, lies between Orpen, Satara and Letaba rest camps.

Left: The restaurant and bar at Satara.
Above: Knobthorn acacias have pretty cream flowers during the late summer.
Top: Evening falls over Satara.

Accommodation

Chalets The two- and three-bed bungalows all have bathrooms and make use of communal kitchen facilities. There are also two- and three-bed bungalows with fully equipped kitchenettes. One luxury bungalow accommodates two, but also has a sleeper couch in the lounge, a bathroom and kitchen. Guest cottages sleep six and have bathrooms as well as fully equipped kitchenettes. The Wells, Rudy Frankel and Stanley guesthouses sleep six, eight and nine respectively and all have bathrooms and fully equipped kitchens.

Camping and caravanning Sites are not allocated so it pays to get in early and claim a shady spot or a site along the fence, depending on your preferences. Communal bathrooms are conveniently situated, as are the kitchens, which have the standard two-plate electric stoves, washing sinks and an instant boiling water dispenser.

Wildlife

The camp It is well worth checking the small water hole near the fence as an array of game, including zebra, wildebeest, waterbuck and warthog, are regularly seen drinking here, as are giraffe and elephant on occasion. Baboons and vervet monkeys regularly wander about the place, making mischief.

The surroundings The grassy plains surrounding Satara are home to large herds of grazers and zebra, waterbuck, wildebeest and buffalo are common. This, in turn, means there are large numbers of predators in the region. The H7 towards Orpen Gate is good for cheetah and sable. The game-viewing board in camp is always chock-a-block with coloured pins.

The Big Five Although rhino can prove a little tricky to spot, all other members of the Big Five occur in large numbers, especially lion. Satara is surrounded by some of the highest lion densities in the park. Leopard are regularly seen.

Birds Look out for red-billed buffalo weaver, thick-billed weaver, red-billed hornbill, African mourning dove, groundscraper thrush, greater blue-eared and Burchell's starlings; in summer, woodland kingfisher. Lesser masked weaver and little swift occur near reception and black crake are found in the little pond. At night, listen out for the purring small engine call of the square-tailed (Mozambique) nightjar and and the deep grunt of Verreaux's (giant) eagle owl. Other owls to look for include barn, African scops and pearl-spotted owl. Montague's and pallid harriers are occasionally seen patrolling the skies over the open plains around the camp after summer rains.

Don't miss!

Satara must be one of the best places in Kruger to spot the big cats. There is a new swimming pool, day centre and water hole with a webcam.

Activities

Morning, sunset and night drives, as well as morning and afternoon guided bushwalks are all on offer at Satara. Wildlife documentaries are shown in the open-air auditorium, weather permitting. The **Mananga 4x4 Adventure Trail** ambles through the plains surrounding the camp and offers an exciting departure from the traditional roads of Kruger. You must have your own 4x4, however, and are required to book at reception on the morning you wish to undertake the drive (see page 163).

Best drives

Satara is one of the prime game-viewing camps in Kruger and a number of good game-viewing roads radiate from the camp.

Timbavati Picnic Site Loop This is possibly one of the most ecologically diverse routes in the central region of the park, passing through no fewer than six different ecozones. As you drive you will see knobthorn/marula savanna, stunted knobthorn savanna on basalt, Olifants rugged veld on rhyolite/basalt, mixed bushwillow woodlands on granite/gneiss, thornveld on gabbro and Delagoa thorn thickets on Ecca shales. From camp, head back to the H1-4 and turn south, almost immediately taking the right-hand turn-off onto the H7 (Satara Road). This heads west through open grassy plains scattered with knobthorns and marula trees. Continue past the turn-off to the S40 on the right, stopping at the **Nsemani Dam**. Although this is a little far from the road, you can get good views of hippo in the water and waterbuck on the banks. In addition there is always an interesting collection of birdlife, such as kingfishers, herons and plovers and general game surrounding the water. It's a favourite drinking spot for wildebeest, zebra, waterbuck and the occasional shy nyala.

Further west, turn right at the S39, heading north along the Timbavati

HEY, DUDE, IT'S IN THE GRASS...

Not that I've tried it myself, you understand, but the terms sweet and sour grass do not actually refer to the taste of the grass. Rather, they refer to its nutrient content.

Grasses growing on nutrient-poor soils (such as those derived from old granite) do not receive sufficient nitrogen from the soil and, by the end of the growing season, do not contain sufficient nutrients to sustain grazing herbivores. This grass is therefore termed sour and harbours far fewer species of grazer. On nutrient-rich soils (such as the basalt corridor throughout Kruger and the red rhyolite soils on the eastern Lebombo fringe) grasses receive plenty of nutrients and are therefore nutritious throughout their growth cycle. Consequently, sweet grass is able to sustain higher densities of grazing herbivores.

The Mananga 4x4 Adventure Trail wanders through grassy plains north of Satara.

River and passing through mixed woodlands of various bushwillow species and knobthorns, while large jackalberries and leadwoods tower over the river course. The **Timbavati Picnic Site** has toilets, gas cookers for hire, cold drinks on sale and shaded tables and chairs, so this is a good spot at which to stop and take a break before continuing east along the S127 back to the H1-4. Head south from here, keeping an eye open as this road always delivers interesting sightings – elephant and buffalo, as well as lion.

Satara Road The Satara Road to **Orpen Gate** is another option to the west of camp. Continue along the H7 (Satara Road) past the S39 turn-off (see above) all the way to Orpen Camp, also passing **Bobbejaans Krans**, 4 km from the turn-off to the S39. This offers a fantastic view over a steeply incised bank of the Timbavati River and, although it is a little far off to see wildlife, the

scenery makes it a special place to stop. This entire route is 'productive', with elephant, zebra, wildebeest and waterbuck widespread. Lion, cheetah and sable are seen relatively often near the turn-off to the Tamboti Tented Camp, 2 km from Orpen Gate.

For a change, on the return journey take the S106 loop past **Rabelais' Hut** – site of the old Rabelais Gate (1926–1954) named after the farm on which it was sited. Further along the S106, it's worth stopping at the **Rabelais Dam** for a while as this often provides visitors in summer with interesting sightings of elephant swimming to cool themselves and shouldn't be missed.

After returning to the tar, continue along until you get to the S12 loop around the **Nsemani Dam**. This short detour often produces worthwhile sightings, including lion and leopard.

Nwanetsi Picnic Site Loop From the camp, take the S100 dirt road east.

SATARA REST CAMP
Tel 013-735-6306/7
Mobile 082-802-1209

Orpen Gate
48 km

This follows the course of the Nwanetsi River and is ranked by many as one of the most rewarding roads in the park's central regions, with regular sightings of lion, elephant, buffalo and leopard. When you reach the S41 (Gudzani Road), head north a short distance to the **Gudzani Dam** just to see if there is any activity there before turning back and heading south. This road runs along the eastern boundary of the plains at the foot of the Lebombo Mountains, before eventually intersecting with the H6. Here you can turn left for the **Nwanetsi Picnic Site** (toilets, gas for hire, basic cold drinks on sale, chairs and tables under shade and washing facilities). A short walk up from the main picnic area is a small thatched viewing point overlooking the Nwanetsi River. This is a pleasant place to spend a few hours and provides good bird-watching as numerous species (fish eagle, malachite and pied kingfisher, squacco heron, reed and white-breasted cormorant, goliath heron, and various swallows,

swifts and martins) are drawn to the water below – this is a little distant so you'll need binoculars. Hornbills and glossy starlings will keep you entertained, but also check the deep shade in the tree canopy for small raptors such as little sparrowhawk and shikra (little banded goshawk). In summer, look for blue-cheeked bee-eater hawking from branches of semi-submerged trees along the waterway. Return to the H1-3 along the H6 tar road, which again often provides great sightings. Alternatively, and if you are up to a very long drive, you can take the S37 (Trichardt Road) further south from the Nwanetsi Picnic Site.

Trichardt Road Heading south from the Nwanetsi Picnic Site, the S37 (Trichardt Road) passes the **Sweni Hide** and view point, overlooking a small pool on the Sweni River, which makes a good alternative to the busier Nwanetsi Picnic Site. Unfortunately, you can leave your vehicle only to enter the hide and there are no picnic facili-

THE ORPENS

In 1935, JH Orpen surveyed the western boundary of the park without pay, while his son, James, was responsible for the layout and design of Shingwedzi Camp. Not to be outdone by the male half of the family, Eileen Orpen purchased seven adjoining farms, totalling 24 529 hectares, which she donated to the park between 1935 and 1944. Today the Orpen name is honoured with a dam and gate/rest camp, while an official plaque on the busy H1-2 commemorates the addition of the seven donated farms.

ties – but you could munch on a biscuit while taking in the interesting bird and animal life that congregate here. On view may be malachite and pied kingfishers, black crake, white-fronted bee-eater and dusky flycatcher, which hawk insects from perches over the water.

After the hide, the road follows the Sweni River for a short while, before leaving the river after which sightings generally slacken off. If you are short of time, pass the turn-off to the S35 (Lindanda Road) as it is a sizeable detour. It was along this road that a lion attacked ranger Harry Wolhuter, while he was returning from a patrol in 1903. He escaped after killing the lion with his sheath knife (see page 67).

Both the S35 and the S37 road take you back to the H1-3 tar road north, which is usually an exciting drive. Large herds of buffalo often occur in the region and lion are frequently spotted. Do not miss the S86 (**Nwaswitsontso Loop**), about 3 km north of the S37 intersection, as this is a lion hot spot.

Waterbuck (above) are almost always found close to water, while steenbok (top) are found throughout the park.

Talamati
Bush Camp

13

Central Region

Talamati offers guests excellent game viewing. It is situated on the banks of the Nwaswitsontso River in a quiet corner in the west of the park near the border with the Manyaleti Private Nature Reserve. Game is prolific in the area, yet the camp is far enough from any large rest camps so you can enjoy your sightings without the crowds. There are two hides in camp and if you are patient, or lucky, sable, leopard, waterbuck and a host of other animals arrive to drink. It is a special corner of the park and it is hard to depart its friendly surrounds without a tug of regret.

Above: Saddle-billed stork are eagerly sought after by birders.
Left: Talamati is shaded and quiet, with comfortable cottages.

Lion prides are often seen on night drives from Talamati.

Accommodation

Chalets The four fully equipped cottages, complete with bathrooms and kitchenettes, sleep four; two beds in one bedroom and two bench beds in the lounge. Guest cottages sleep six in two bedrooms with two beds each and another two on bench beds in the lounge. Double beds are available in some units.

Wildlife

The camp There are two hides. The hide nearer reception overlooks a water hole and boasts activity throughout the day. Leopard also sometimes drink at the water's edge so keep a lookout. In the dry season, sable drink here regularly. Walk in quietly and consider others.

The surroundings The grassy plains, with mixed combretum and acacia thornveld, mean that a diverse selection of wildlife occurs in the region. Grazers such as zebra and wildebeest are common, as are browsers such as kudu. There are big lion prides in the area that often lie around on the roads in the early mornings and evenings. Leopard are often seen along the river courses, especially during the dry winter months.

The Big Five With the exception of rhino, the Big Five are commonly seen near the camp. For rhinos, head south.

Birds Talamati is good for several woodland species, including cuckoos, kingfishers and rollers, while narina trogons have been seen in the trees lining the nearby river course. Several stork species are common at the water hole beneath the hide nearest reception.

Don't miss!

Spend time in the hide overlooking the water hole near reception as there is always something going on – highlights are the sable and leopard that often come down to drink, especially in the dry winter months.

Activities

Morning and sunset guided drives (in a 10-seat vehicle) and early-morning guided bushwalks (which include a break for a light snack) can all be booked at reception.

Best drives

It is well worth patrolling the Nwaswitsontso River along the S145 and S140 respectively as both are extremely rewarding when it comes to game-viewing. If you want to drive further, see 'Best drives' in Orpen (page 76) and Satara (page 80).

Nwaswitsontso Loop Follow the S145 (Talamati Road) east to the intersection with the S36 (Nhlanguleni Road) and turn south to the **Ngwenyeni Water Hole**. Hippo, waterbuck, crocodile and other game are always found in the area. From here, continue south to the **Nhlanguleni Picnic Site** (this road can be very quiet, however) or retrace your steps to the turn-off east onto the S125 (Nwaswitsontso Road). This follows the course of the river of the same name and often delivers lion, elephant, and good general game. At the H1-3 tar road, head north, stopping off at **Nkaya Pan**, which

BIRD-HIDE ETIQ

Try to arrive as quie, sible and, once in the . noise and movement to . mum. Be patient – birds sp by your arrival will often retur, once everything settles down.

If you are a serious twitcher, pack plenty of refreshments to fortify your stay.

Remember to turn off your cellphone, or you're likely to be lynched by any of the well-fortified twitchers mentioned above!

is often busy with game. Rhino are commonly reported, as are lion, leopard and elephant, especially in the late afternoon. Return to the tar and, 7 km further north, turn left onto the S126 (Sweni Road), which follows the Sweni River and is renowned for good sightings of leopard and often large prides of lion. At the intersection of the S126 and the S36, turn left and stop off at the well-serviced **Muzandzeni Picnic Site**. Large herds of elephant and general game are often seen at **Shimangwaneni Dam** and it is well worth spending some time here before heading south to complete the loop, returning to camp along the S145. This loop is good for sable and often produces sightings of large lion prides.

Roodewal Bush Camp
Central Region

Named after the striking red walls of the rock intrusion that runs north–south nearby, Roodewal – from the Dutch meaning 'red wall' – is a shady private camp accommodating 19 guests and overlooking the Timbavati River. There are no restaurant, shopping or administration facilities in camp and it can be booked only as a whole by a single party, which must check in at either Olifants or Satara. It is peaceful and quiet, allowing you to escape to your very own bit of bushveld for a while.

African scops owls are often seen from the deck at Roodewal.

Accommodation

Chalets This small camp has four separate units: one four-bed, fully equipped family unit and three five-bed huts, each with a shower and toilet. There is a communal, stand-alone kitchen with two fridges and stove, four braai stands but, with the exception of one attendant, no other facilities. Guests are expected to bring their own supplies and do their own cooking. The nearest shops are at Satara and Olifants rest camps, so it is best to come well stocked.

Wildlife

The camp The magnificent trees lining the banks of the Timbavati River attract large numbers of baboons and monkeys, as well as birds. African scops, as well as pearl-spotted and barred owlet are common in camp.

The surroundings Immediately opposite the camp are two water holes, Roodewal and Goedgegun, which attract an interesting array of game such as impala, kudu, wildebeest and zebra. There are usually plenty of giraffe in the area.

The Big Five You should have no problem seeing the Big Five from Roodewal, with the possible exception of rhino, which may require driving into the southern regions of the park. Lion are common near Satara and leopard are often seen along the Timbavati River. A good place to find elephant is the **Piet Grobler Dam**, where they often drink. Buffalo are encountered most frequently north of Satara. Elephant and lion also frequent the area.

Birds The giant trees lining the river shade the camp and harbour crested and black-collared barbet, grey-headed parrot, African and diderick cuckoo and red-capped (Natal) robin-chat.

Don't miss!

Roodewal is the perfect foil for the frantic pace of modern life and there is nothing like a quiet morning sitting on the deck overlooking the course of the Timbavati River, even if it is dry. Based at Roodewal, you should also be able to tick at least four of the Big Five (see above), while sightings of impala, kudu, wildebeest, zebra and birds such as the two bushveld tchagras – black-crowned and brown-crowned (three-streaked) – and various other woodland species are common.

Activities

Guided outings are offered at Roodewal, although it is imperative that these are booked well in advance, preferably when making your reservation, as there are no guides or rangers stationed at the camp.

Best drives

Roodewal is situated on the S39 (Timbavati Road), which follows the course of the Timbavati River in a north–south direction. This limits your routes to a degree, but game in the area is generally very good and if you want more options you need only drive a short distance before the S39 intersects with the greater road network (notably, the H1-4 south and the H1-5 north) giving you a far greater choice.

Bangu Water Hole Head north on the S39, past the **Roodewal** and **Goedgegun water holes** along the

red-rock walls of the dyke, crossing over the H1-4 onto the S89 (Ngotso Weir Road). Cheetah and lion occur along this road regularly, so keep your eyes open. When you reach the S90, turn south, continuing slowly along this road until you reach the Bangu Water Hole. Here zebra and wildebeest often congregate to drink, and lion and cheetah are often reported. It is not worth continuing along the S90 much further, so retrace your steps back to the S89 turn-off.

If you want a change of scenery for the drive home, keep on the S90 heading north and, after the road crosses the Olifants River at the low bridge, turn left onto the S91. It is worth pausing a while on the bridge as often there are great sightings along the river course. In particular, birders should keep their eyes open as both Pel's fishing owl and white-crowned lapwing have been spotted. Continue along the S91 as it hugs the river, whose banks are lined

Above: Double-banded sandgrouse are seen along dirt roads. Top: Remember your table manners ... we're on camera.

with sycamore figs, giant leadwoods, jackalberries and fever trees. Turn south onto the H1-5 for home.

Timbavati Picnic Site Heading south, follow the S39 (Timbavati Road) along the river, stopping at the **Piet Grobler Dam** to the west, as there are always hippos, crocodiles and a collection of water birds about. Elephant, kudu, waterbuck and giraffe are also common. A kilometre or so further is

ROODEWAL BUSH LODGE

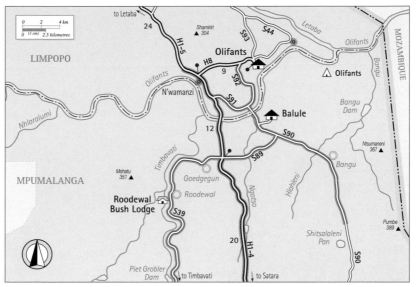

the **Sasol-Ratelpan Hide**, overlooking a small pool. Good sightings of hippo and large crocodiles sunning themselves on the bank are possible from the hide, as well as squacco heron, little bittern, black crake, pied kingfisher, reed and white-breasted cormorant and goliath heron, among others.

Stop at the attractive **Timbavati Picnic Site**, where you can hire gas cookers, buy a limited range of cold drinks and enjoy a break in the shade on the tables provided as you watch the tame bushbuck wander by. From here, you can return along the S127 (Mthomeni Road), which takes you east to the H1-4, or retrace your steps along the S39. The H1-4 passes through open grasslands north of Satara – a prime game-viewing area, so this is possibly the best option. As you head north, keep your eyes open for lion, elephant,

Southern ground hornbill can regularly be seen along the H1-4.

buffalo, zebra, wildebeest and a host of other game. It's worth stopping off at the **Ngotso Dam** as this attracts good game, often providing excellent sightings of hippo, elephant and waterbuck. Return to Roodewal along the S39.

Olifants

Central Region

15

Perched on a cliff overlooking the Olifants River, this rest camp (one of the smallest but most popular: occupies the most scenic location in Kruger. If you book early enough you can even get a bungalow right on the edge of the cliff and can spend your evenings with the Lowveld at your feet. The camp has more to offer than its view, however, and is ideally situated – near the confluence of the Letaba and Olifants rivers – for great game-viewing and interesting birding. Moreover, the camp's central location allows you to strike deep into the mopane shrubveld of the north and the game-rich central plains to the south.

From Olifants' view site, overlooking the Olifants River way below, you feel as if you have the entire Lowveld at your feet.

Accommodation

Chalets The three-bed bungalows either make use of the communal kitchens or contain a small kitchenette; four-bed bungalows have two bedrooms (one has two bathrooms) and a small kitchenette. The two guesthouses, Lebombo and Nshawu, each sleep eight people and are fully equipped. Always check when booking whether your unit has crockery and cutlery, because some do not – in which case, they can be hired for a small fee.

Camping and caravanning No sites are available in camp, but are at nearby Balule Satellite Camp.

Wildlife

The camp From the deck overlooking the Olifants River, you can see a range of animals drinking at the river below – elephant, waterbuck and impala are common, while large crocodile and lots of hippo are usually visible in the pools. Thick-tailed galago (bushbabies), fruit bats, vervet monkey and baboon are always present in camp.

The surroundings Game-viewing is exceptional along the Olifants and Letaba rivers, and improves as you move south into the grassland areas around Satara. In particular, the **Bangu Water Hole** often offers fantastic sightings and it is always worth checking this area, perhaps best known for its pair of resident cheetah.

The Big Five All members of the Big Five are present in the area; buffalo and elephant are common, but you may have to scratch around to see rhino. Lion are common south of camp and leopard are often seen in the

densely wooded river valleys.

Birds If you are keen on birds, the River Walk ups your chances of seeing the teddy-bear lookalike Pel's fishing owl. White-fronted plover and white-crowned lapwing also frequent the sandbanks of the Olifants River and there have been occasional sightings of white-backed night heron and the very rare black egret in the area. Both black and saddle-billed stork breed in the vicinity. In summer, bats attract gabar goshawk, Eurasian hobby and bat hawk at sunset. In camp you will find red-winged starling, yellow-bellied greenbul, mocking cliff-chat and a variety of sunbirds.

Don't miss!

Guided mountain biking trail, the River Walk and sundowners from the deck, and the astronomy drive for a talk on the African skies and telescope viewing.

Activities

Of the many guided walks in the area, special mention should be made of the **River Walk** option. This follows thick vegetation along the banks of the Olifants River and provides visitors with the chance of seeing the rare Pel's fishing owl, as well as hippo, crocodile and so on. A resident leopard is sometimes seen. Morning and evening guided walks are offered; if you're lucky, these sometimes offer up the Big Five.

Currently, Olifants is the only camp that offers **mountain bike trails**. There are three routes. The first is a very gentle afternoon outride down to the river, where you can enjoy a snack under the wary eyes of the nearby hippos that

Book early enough to get one of the units on the fence for magnificent views.

survey you balefully from the water and offer up snorts of disgust every so often. The longer and more technical **Olifants/ Letaba Confluence Trail,** which – as the name suggests – takes you into a region bordered by these two majestic rivers. Lastly, the taxing **Mozambique Border Trail** takes you east, towards the Lebombo Mountains, for most of a day and requires both technical ability and fitness. The price includes the services of two armed guards, bikes, helmets and mid-ride snacks.

Best drives

Olifants is situated at the transition between three ecozones: the rocky Lebombo Mountain Bushveld to the east, the monotonous Mopane Shrubveld to the north and the open grassy plains and mixed acacia and bushwillow of the Olifants Rugged Veld to the south. This provides diverse habitats for visitors to explore; a number of excellent roads radiate out from the camp.

Letaba River Route About 1 km east from the gate along the H8, take the S93 dirt road north, and almost immediately turn right onto the S44. This gently undulating dirt road follows the course of the Olifants River to the **Olifants Viewpoint** overlooking a majestic sweeping bend of the river. There are always hippo in the permanent pools below and through your binoculars you will often get good sightings of a host of other game, such as kudu, waterbuck and giraffe, as they come down to the river to drink. Unfortunately, the animals are a little too far off for good wildlife photographs. Continue north, following the Letaba River now, where you are likely to encounter buffalo, elephant, kudu and other game species. If you are lucky, you may even spot lion and leopard in the riverine vegetation. This is one of the most common areas in the park to see kills.

You can continue all the way along past the **Engelhard Dam** to Letaba for lunch, and then it is worth continuing on to the **Matambeni Hide** overlook-

. Dam first, where you
.dile, hippo and elephant
ge, not to mention a pleth-
.ater birds: greater flamingo,
..'s and three-banded plover,
.le-billed stork, black crake, bittern,
.omb (knob-billed) duck and others.
Alternatively, turn left onto the S46,
which heads west to the H1-5 tar road.
The H1-5 can be a little quiet initially
but as you approach the Olifants River
again, things generally hot up, with
elephant, buffalo, lion, leopard, kudu,
giraffe and other sightings common.

Olifants River Loop About 2km
east from camp along the H8, take the
S92 south. This hugs the Olifants River,
passing through open mixed grasslands
interrupted by knobthorns, euphorbias
and various bushwillow and clusterleaf
species as it meanders along. Numerous
turn-offs provide views over the river
lined with sycamore figs, leadwoods
and fever trees. You are likely to see fish
eagles; lion and leopard are common,
while elephant, buffalo, giraffe, waterbuck and other game are nearly always
present. Elephant are especially prolific
in this area, which harbours some of the
park's biggest tuskers. Another 7km on,
there is a turn-off to the S90, which
heads south, crossing the Olifants (see
below), but continue along the S91 until
it reaches the H1-4 where you can head
north to the **Nwamanzi Viewpoint**.
This provides a sweeping view over
the Olifants River and, often, great
game sightings, including elephant,
waterbuck, kudu, buffalo and giraffe.
Alternatively, follow the H1-4 south as
it heads towards Satara.

S90 to Bangu This is another prime

> ## KNOBTHORNS
> One of the dominant features of
> the bushveld landscape south
> of the Olifants River is the proli-
> feration of knobthorn acacias
> (*Acacia nigrescens*). These burst
> into flower – pale yellow, feath-
> ery fingers – from August to
> September, usually before the
> leaves reappear. At this time, the
> landscape for as far as the eye
> can see takes on a distinct
> yellow hue. Knobthorns are
> named after the large knobs that
> form on the trunk and young
> branches of the tree, designed
> to prevent damage from grazing.
> That said, knobthorns are impor-
> tant browsing trees and a host of
> antelope make use of the leaves
> and flowers. It's a favourite of
> giraffes too. They wrap their
> long, thick tongues around the
> heavily armed branchlets and
> pull ... stripping off the leaves.

game-viewing route. Follow the S90
from the S92 and cross the Olifants
River on the low-level bridge. From the
bridge you often have great sightings,
so it's worth pausing a while to scan
the banks for animals, such as elephant,
waterbuck, terrapin, crocodile and
hippo. White-crowned lapwing, greater
painted snipe and Pel's fishing owl
are sometimes seen here in the early
morning and at last light. Continue
past the turn to **Balule Caravan Camp**,
after which the S90 passes through
Olifants Rugged Veld characterised by
knobthorn acacias, purplepod cluster-

leaf and various species of bushwillow with mixed grasses that attract giraffe, kudu, elephant, wildebeest and zebra. A few kilometres later the environment changes to open grassy areas studded with knobthorns, leadwoods and acacias as you head towards **Bangu Water Hole**. Wildlife can be prolific

around the water hole, with large herds of zebra and wildebeest congregating in the dry season. Lion and cheetah are common in the area. After the immediate surrounds of the water hole, sightings tend to be less frequent, so it's best to turn and retrace your steps. One option for the return is to cut across to the H1-4 on the S89 (Ngotso Weir Road). This route often boasts wild dog and cheetah, while the H1-4 between the S89 and H8 turn-off back to camp is also renowned for good sightings, especially as you enter the lush Olifants River valley.

South towards Satara The H1–4 towards Satara can be extremely rewarding, as this heads into the open grassy areas frequented by herds of wildebeest and zebra. Lion and cheetah are regularly encountered along the route, while buffalo, elephant and other

Above: The famous tusks on Olifants Gate have now been replaced with models.
Top: White-backed vultures often survey the plains south of Olifants.

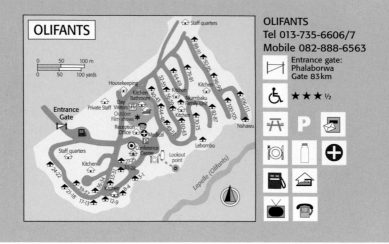

OLIFANTS

OLIFANTS
Tel 013-735-6606/7
Mobile 082-888-6563

Entrance gate:
Phalaborwa
Gate 83 km

★★★½

game are common. You can follow the road all the way to Satara, passing the string of water holes along the road, all acting as magnets for game. It's worth taking the detour to the **Ngotso Dam** as this relatively large body of water is populated with hippo and crocodile, and water birds including comb (knob-billed) duck, three-banded plover and, if you're lucky, saddle-billed stork.

Alternatively, turn west onto the S127 (Mthomeni Road) and head out to the **Timbavati Picnic Site** for lunch (gas for hire, basic cold drinks on sale and tables and chairs). From here, head north again, following the S39 (Timbavati Road) along the Timbavati River. After the Skukuza–Sabie area, this is the next best for leopard sightings. About 4,5 km after the picnic site is the **Sasol-Ratelpan Hide**, which overlooks a small reed-enclosed pool. Good sightings of hippo are possible from here, and large crocodile sun themselves on the banks nearby. The

hide faces west, but it is a little far off for great wildlife pictures. A little further, there is a turn to the left to a viewpoint overlooking the **Piet Grobler Dam**. Hippo, crocodile and waterbuck are abundant, while general game congregate here to drink.

The S39 continues north through attractive open countryside on one side and dense river vegetation on the other, providing you with excellent opportunities to see bushbuck, elephant, zebra, wildebeest, kudu, waterbuck, giraffe and a diversity of birds, including grassland species such as various francolin and spurfowl, black-bellied and kori bustard and forest species such as scaly-throated honeyguide, grey-headed parrot, grey-headed kingfisher and bush-shrike. The **Roodewal** and **Goedgegun water holes**, shortly after the turn-off to Roodewal Rest Camp, often offer good sightings as zebra, wildebeest, kudu, impala and often elephant and giraffe congregate in the area to drink.

Balule Rustic Camp

16

Central Region

This very small satellite camp in the Olifants River valley, a short distance from where the S90 crosses the Olifants River, started life as one of the few camps where people of all races were allowed to visit during the apartheid era. Those days are behind us, however, and Balule has become a firm favourite of those wanting a no-frills, back-to-basics camping or bungalow experience. It is also a great spot if you are hoping to catch a glimpse of the shy Pel's fishing owl as these are seen relatively often near the camp.

Although Balule is predominantly for caravans and camping, small rondavels are available.

Don't let the big animals, such as Burchell's zebra (left), grab all your attention or you'll miss the small attractions of the park, such as the impala lily (right).

Accommodation

All visitors check in at either Olifants or Satara rest camps.

Chalets Six small, three-person huts use communal facilities. It's a strictly self-catering, braaiing camp.

Camping and caravanning There are pleasant, shady, ungrassed sites, many of which look out on the perimeter fence. Sites are not allocated and electric boxes with the standard caravan fittings are scattered throughout.

Wildlife

The camp Keep a lookout along the fence at night as hyena regularly visit in search of scraps. A pair of Pel's fishing owls frequents the tall trees lining the river here and they are seen occasionally from camp. The resident fish eagles also fill the landscape with their call.

The surroundings The camp is well situated to strike north and south into the park, allowing you to access a range of ecozones. South of the camp you are very likely to see lion and other preda-

tors. Cheetah are common near Bangu. North of the camp you are certain to see elephant and large buffalo herds.

The Big Five All of the Big Five are regularly seen from the camp, although rhino may require some looking.

Birds Greater painted snipe, Pel's fishing owl, white-crowned lapwing and white-fronted plover are all seen along the Olifants River.

Don't miss!

The Pel's fishing owl is one of the most sought-after birds for twitchers and it is well worth keeping a watch on the river near camp in the evening.

Activities

On offer at Balule are morning, sunset and night drives, as well as morning and afternoon river walks, and mountain-bike trails, all of which may be booked at reception at Olifants Camp.

Best drives

See Olifants Camp (page 95).

Letaba
Central Region

17

Sited on a sweeping bend of the wide, sandy Letaba River – the Sotho word *lehlaba* means 'sand river' – this is many people's preferred base in the park. The camp follows typical old-style SANParks architecture and is one of the camps that has defined Kruger for many South Africans. Its position is ideal, enabling you to access the mopane veld to the north and the densely populated game areas further south. The camp is shady and comfortable, with large mahogany and apple-leaf trees shielding you from the sun's onslaught, while spacious grassy areas surrounding the accommodation units allow the kids to enjoy themselves with gusto.

Above: Buffalo are naturally curious and if you sit patiently they often walk right by your vehicle.
Top: In camp don't miss the excellent elephant museum.

Accommodation

Chalets Most of the two- and three-bed units have been upgraded so few now share ablution or kitchen facilities. A newly opened day centre includes its own swimming pool, kiosk and braai places.

Guest cottages sleep six in separate bedrooms and also have fully equipped kitchenettes. There are also two multi-roomed guesthouses – Fish Eagle, sleeping eight, and Melville, sleeping nine.

Safari tents The two- and four-bed safari tents both come equipped with a fridge but visitors use communal ablutions and kitchens.

Camping and caravanning Letaba has a large sandy camping area with plenty of shade, pleasant communal ablutions and communal kitchens with two-plate electric hobs, washing facilities and instant hot-water dispensers.

Wildlife

The camp Wonderful old trees – ilala palms, sycamore figs, coral trees and leadwoods – shade the camp and attract a host of birdlife, including brown-headed parrot and black-headed oriole. Bushbuck graze the lawns and it is not uncommon to see pythons in close proximity to camp. It is also worth spending time at the restaurant, with its magnificent view over the Letaba River where elephant and waterbuck, among others, are often seen drinking, especially during the dry winter months when surface water away from the main river courses dries up.

The surroundings A pride of about 15 lions frequents the area, as does a resident leopard, making this a good

A few kilometres from camp along the S95 is an old leadwood with a Portuguese cross carved in the bark. It was apparently carved by Diocleciano Fernandes das Neves in 1860–61 while en route to the Soutpansberg during an exploratory trek from the Portuguese port of Lourenço Marques.

camp from which to see these two sought-after predators. General game, such as kudu, impala, waterbuck and bushbuck, is good in the area due to the proximity of the river and dense riverine vegetation.

The Big Five Rhino can be difficult to spot, but all other members of the Big Five are regularly seen around Letaba. The area is particularly good for elephant and buffalo, which occur in large numbers in the region.

Birds Birding at Letaba is rewarding throughout the year; it is rich in species and some birds are particularly confiding and habituated to humans, which makes for good photography. One of these species is the African mourning dove, which is seen only in camp and not in the surrounding bushveld.

All the small owls occur in camp and it's worth asking around if anyone has seen pearl-spotted, barred and African scops owl. At night, the owl calls are supplemented by calls from both square-tailed (Mozambique) and fiery-necked nightjar, as well as water thick-knee. The floods in February 2000 unfortunately devasted much of the river frontage and affected the habitat of birds that lived in dense riverine vegetation. In summer, look out for the red-headed weaver and collared (red-

LETABA REST CAMP

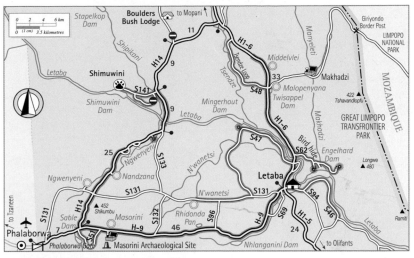

The flying banana – also known as a yellow-billed hornbill.

winged) pratincole in the surrounding areas. Red-billed oxpeckers nest in the tall ilala palms near the restaurant.

Don't miss!

A fascinating collection of information and displays is contained in the **Letaba Elephant Hall**. Also in the museum is information on the 'Magnificent Seven', Kruger's legendary old tuskers.

Activities

Morning and afternoon guided bush-walks are booked at reception as are morning, sunset and night drives. Wildlife documentaries are shown in the open-air auditorium every evening, weather permitting.

Best drives

Even though this is one of the largest camps in the park, the large number of routes in the vicinity means that you will probably not encounter as many other visitors on individual routes as you might expect.

Tsendze Loop Follow the H1-6 tar

road north, crossing the high-level bridge over the sandy Letaba River and continue on, keeping an eye out for lion, which are often seen in the area during the early mornings and evenings. It is also good for kudu and waterbuck. Take the left-hand turn onto the S48 (**Tsendze Loop**), about 13 km from the bridge. Initially, game sightings are infrequent but after the road hits the river, things can get interesting. When you reach the H1-6 again you can either head back along the tar, or retrace your steps and repeat the Tsendze Loop. If you head south on the tarred H1-6, keep an eye out around **Middelvlei Water Hole**, where you often find mixed herds of zebra and wildebeest. Lion are also seen regularly in the area.

Northern Engelhard Dam This attractive route, which meanders through lush vegetation on the north bank of the Letaba River, alternating with mopane veld, offers fantastic game-viewing opportunities. Head north on the H1-6 and, after crossing the high-level bridge over the Letaba River (look out for little swifts and bats that breed and roost under the arches), turn right on to the S62. Stop as often as you can on the short turn-offs from the road down to the river.

About 5 km along the S62, there is a turn-off to the right, which leads to the **Matambeni Hide**, overlooking the **Engelhard Dam**. Time spent here can be very rewarding, especially if you want to see the hippo, crocodile and elephant which browse along the vegetated banks and occasionally swim, especially during hot summer afternoons.

Letaba has a comfortable day-visitors' area and is well signposted.

Birds such as greater flamingo, Kittlitz's plover, comb (knob-billed) duck, little bittern and others are common. Also look out for the collared (red-wing) pratincole that breed near here. Back on the S62, it continues on to a great viewpoint overlooking the dam where a collection of water birds, crocodile and hippo are usually seen. The road then climbs the slopes of Longwe Hill (479 m) to **Engelhard Lookout**, which looks west over the Engelhard Dam and Letaba Valley.

Mingerhout Dam Road Head north along the H1-6, but turn left onto the S47 (Letaba River Road) before you reach the high-water bridge over the Letaba River. The road hugs the southern banks of the Letaba, crossing the little N'wanetsi Stream where you can often see terrapins and a particularly bold three-banded plover, which comes within metres of your vehicle if you sit patiently at close range. The road continues on to the **Mingerhout Dam**, where a little turnout provides you with a good view over the dam and river. Unfortunately, this lookout is a little too far from the action to get good photos or great animal sightings. Lion, elephant and buffalo are seen relatively often along the S47. From the dam, the loop heads south into a bland mopane-carpeted landscape, although there is a chance of seeing large buffalo herds as well as elephant. At the T-junction with the S131, turn left to return to Letaba, or go right and continue west for a longer full-day drive to **Masorini**.

Phalaborwa/Masorini A number of different routes head west towards the Phalaborwa Gate, allowing you to explore various options, particularly on weekends when the main H-9 tar road can be busy with day visitors.

The H-9 follows the course of the Nhlanganini River and, although the scenery is a little monotonous, every so often it is broken by loops to pretty water holes and granite koppies. It is well worth taking the S69 loop to **Nhlanganini Water Hole** 2 km from the crossroads with the main H1-6/H1-5 running north–south. This often offers interesting sightings, including saddle-billed stork and other water birds. By taking this loop, you will

Safari tents are convenient, comfortable and affordable.

miss the turn to the S131, however, and should continue along the H-9 at least as far as the right turn onto the S96 immediately after the pretty 414m granite koppie, **Shilawuri**. Here you have two options. Stick to the H9, or continue along the S96 and head north to the S131 dirt road that runs parallel to this. There is very little advantage to this, unless the H9 is too busy for your taste, in which case the S131 is gener-

There's nothing much better than brunch after a successful morning game drive.

ally much quieter. The S131 passes two attractive little water holes – **Nwanetsi** and **Shivhulani** – around which you are bound to see a variety of game, such as impala, warthog, kudu and buffalo, as well as water birds such as three-banded plover, African jacana, hamerkop, African spoonbill, moorhen and red-billed teal. At the T-junction with the H14, head south past the attractive **Shikumbu** (494 m) granite koppie, keeping a lookout for klipspringers along the way. At the T-junction with the H-9, head east towards the **Masorini Archaeological Site** or west to the Phalaborwa Gate (see also page 167).

These routes can be a little frustrating as game can be difficult to see in the thick vegetation, but you often see elephant and large herds of buffalo. Lion are common, while the attractive granite koppies are some of the best klipspringer habitat in the park.

Letaba River Route The S46 route begins by skirting the southern banks of the Engelhard Dam and continues south along the Letaba River. It is possibly one of the best early morning or evening drives in the north of the park, and you have a good chance of seeing a wide variety of animals and birds all along the route.

Along the way, you are likely to spot leopard, lion and hyena in the mornings and evenings, while herds of elephant, impala, kudu, waterbuck, warthog and bushbuck are common in the thick bush throughout the day.

Take the various turnouts overlooking the Engelhard Dam, where you are likely to see hippo, elephant, crocodile and a host of birdlife, such as comb (knob-billed) duck, black crake, little bittern, squacco, goliath and grey heron, black-crowned night heron, moorhen

LETABA

LETABA REST CAMP
Tel 013-735-6636/7
Mobile 082-802-1255

Phalaborwa
Gate 51 km

Above: A three-banded plover. Right: Large buffalo herds are often seen in the area.

and others attracted to this large permanent water source.

The S46 veers west and heads back to the H1-5 tar road, passing through mopane shrubveld. You can continue along the river, however, by taking the S44 south. Where this splits to the S93– right and S44–left, follow the S44 on to the **Olifants Viewpoint** which, as its name suggests, overlooks an attractive sweep of the Olifants River. There is a new Phalaborwa entrance gate plus a new network of roads in this area – ask at reception.

18 Shimuwini Bush Camp

Central Region

Shimuweni is peaceful and unhurried, allowing a true escape from your hectic life.

This attractive bush camp, far from the bustle of everyday Kruger and overlooking the Shimuwini Dam, is one of my favourite places in the park. The staff are friendly and the spacious grassy area outside the bungalows allows plenty of space for the kids to gallop about after a hard day's game-viewing. At the back of the camp, a narrow footpath wanders through an unspoilt area of mopane woodland. It is also well worth spending some time in the hide overlooking the dam before heading up to your evening braai. I love that period of the day as the light slowly fades from the surroundings and the night begins to waken amid a torrent of calls ... hippos begin venturing from the water and the bats start to flitter through the sky on their quest for bugs. Due to its location, game sightings in the area can be a little infrequent; however, when you do stumble across something interesting, you usually have it to yourself.

Accommodation

Chalets The spacious, four-bed cottages have a fully equipped kitchenette. There are also five- and six-bed family cottages with a fully equipped kitchenette, and en-suite bathrooms. The camp has been extensively upgraded, with an added social lapa area with braai stands for social gatherings.

Wildlife

The camp A tame grey duiker wanders about the camp grounds and hippo frequent the Shimuwini Dam overlooked by the camp.

The surroundings There are large numbers of elephant and buffalo in the area and visitors often see leopard. Nyala are also regularly encountered near camp. At night you can hear the whooping of spotted hyena.

The Big Five Lion and rhino are scarce but elephant, buffalo and leopard are regularly sighted.

Birds White-backed night heron, greater painted snipe, Pel's fishing owl and collared (red-wing) pratincole can be seen at Shimuwini Dam, while a number of bushveld and woodland species, such as woodland and grey-hooded (in summer) kingfisher, dusky flycatcher, grey-headed bush shrike and black-crowned tchagra are often seen in the trees that shade the camp.

Don't miss!

The framed black mamba skin at reception ... at 3,3 m, it illustrates the truly awesome size these snakes can reach. Its aggressive behaviour and potent venom make this one of the most feared and dangerous snakes in Africa.

It is fairly common in the bushveld. Also, be sure to be on the lookout in the morning and evening for wild dog on the H9.

Activities

Morning and night drives, morning walks and a combination sundowner walk and night drive are offered, but these should all be booked seven days in advance.

Best drives

Shimuwini is a little isolated and, unfortunately, roads are a little limited. However, it has a private loop of 20 km of gravel road along the Letaba River reserved for residents of the camp.

River Loop If you are after a short morning or evening drive, it is well worth heading out along the river loop, which turns off the S141 main access road 4 km from camp. This provides views over the **Shimuwini Dam** and Letaba River and lion, leopard and elephant are often seen in the area. A special cul de sac allows a close-up of the large baobab (estimated to be thousands of years old) that gives the camp its name (*shimuwini* means 'place of the baobab').

Masorini Archaeological Site An interesting outing from Shimuwini is to the fascinating archaeological site at Masorini Hill. This restored village, with its associated museum, provides visitors with a glance of how indigenous peoples lived before Europeans arrived in the region.

It is a relatively long drive, however, so it might be a good idea to pack a picnic lunch to enjoy at the Masorini

Leopards are regularly seen near camp; hippos in permanent water bodies.

site, where gas cookers can be hired, cold drinks purchased and tables and chairs are available. From the S141, take the H14 south until you reach the T-junction with the H-9. Wild dog are often encountered along this road, especially in the morning and late afternoon pretty much throughout the year. Turn left at the T-junction and continue along through the attractive rounded granite intrusions until you reach the Masorini site. Keep a lookout for klipspringers, which are frequently seen on the granite boulders. For birders, Masorini is one of the few places in the park where you will see familiar chat. Look out for southern black tit, brubru, black-backed puffback, golden-breasted bunting, black cuckooshrike and bushveld pipit. In summer, look for Eurasian golden orioles after rain. Large herds of buffalo are also common. For a change, you can continue along the H-9 until you reach the left-hand turn-off onto the S132 and return that way home, or you can retrace your path heading home along the H14 again.

Boulders
Bush Camp
Central Region

This secluded bush lodge at the foot of a large granite boulder overlooking a private water hole offers visitors a slice of bushveld to call their own. The lodge is comfortable and unfenced – the entire camp is raised on concrete pillars that ensure your safety without compromising on the feeling of true wilderness. Electricity is provided by solar panels and all cooking is done on gas so that no noisy generator interrupts your quiet time. Twelve guests can be accommodated but you have to book the entire lodge. My favourite thing about Boulders is probably that you are left to your own devices ... with only two park staff members in residence, who clean the facilities and service the rooms.

Boulders is unfenced, allowing you to experience wild Africa from your deck chair.

Accommodation

The main unit contains two large bedrooms, each with an en-suite bathroom, one with a bath and the other with a shower. Four other two-bed units, all with bathrooms (bath and shower) make up the rest of the sleeping accommodation.

Wildlife

The camp Kudu, impala, giraffe and a variety of other game visit the water hole, allowing for great sightings from the comfort of your deck chair. At night look for galagos (bushbabies) and listen for nightjars.

The surroundings Zebra, wildebeest, eland, kudu and a collection of other game are all relatively common. This is also a good area for cheetah.

The Big Five You may have to scratch around for lion in this area, although elephant are usually quite easily spotted. Leopard are seen fairly regularly, as are buffalo herds. Rhino are rarely seen but if you do happen to see Ore (with one ear missing), let an official or ranger know.

Birds Boulders is small and quiet, situated in thick mopane and bushwillow woodlands. This means that birds literally flit through camp without noticing you; in particular it is good for African scops and pearl-spotted owl, woodland kingfisher (in summer), grey-headed bushshrike and others.

Elephants generally have right of way on all roads. Are you really going to dispute it?

Don't miss!

Sundowners over your private water hole, watching the parade of wildlife that arrives to take the day's last drink before the busy African night returns. Then head to the fenced-in portion of the boulder koppie behind the camp for a braai. Don't forget to keep a watch out for scavenging hyena attracted by the smell of grilling meat.

Activities

Guided morning, sunset and night drives, as well as guided bushwalks, are possible, but it is imperative that these are booked at the time of making your reservation because guides need to be arranged from Mopani rest camp.

Best drives

Unfortunately, roads are few in the area, so you need to travel relatively large distances to see animals. That said, you could be lucky enough to stumble across awesome sightings on your private access road, so keep your eyes open.

Shongololo Loop (See also Mopani Camp on page 119.) If you do this loop from Boulders it is probably best not to drive the entire route but rather stick to the more productive southern part of the Shongololo Loop, only as far as **Baanbreker Water Hole** (on the S142), turning at the water hole and retracing your steps past the turn-off back to Boulders (the S136) and then on to the **Nshawu Loop**.

Nshawu/Tropic of Capricorn Loop (See also Mopani Camp on page 117.) Follow the S136 access road north and turn right when you reach the S142 Shongololo Loop and head to the H1-6 tar road. Turn right and then left onto the S49 dirt road. Turn left again about 3km further on, heading past the **Mooiplaas Water Hole** and then left yet again once you join the S50 (Nshawu Vlei–Dipene Road), which follows the small Nshawu River. Almost immediately take the right-hand side track down to the **Nshawu Dam** where the road gets relatively

> SANParks bush lodges make an ideal family holiday ... or even better, hook up with some mates for a great Kruger getaway.

close to the water and offers you good views of hippo, crocodile, and all sorts of water birds, including comb (knob-billed) duck, moorhen, Kittlitz's plover, African spoonbill, blacksmith lapwing, and, occasionally, saddle-billed stork. The dam itself is in an open grassy area, often providing good sightings of elephant; tsessebe are sometimes also seen. Many grassland birds are seen here, too, such as Swainson's, Natal, and Shelley's francolin, red-crested and black-bellied korhaan, kori bustard and Montagu's harrier. Return to the S50 road and head north, eventually taking the S143 turn to your left. Follow along this, turning left again at the S144. This takes you back to the H1-6 tar road, passing through a small patch of gabbro soil where the vegetation changes to thornveld for a few kilometres before reverting to mopane. As you head south along the H1-6, keep an eye out for sable, especially near **Bowker's Kop Water Hole**.

Tsendze Loop Head south from Boulders on the S136 and turn left onto the H14 (Mopani–Phalaborwa Road) and then right onto the H1-6. The S48 (the Tsendze Loop) begins about 2km further on. This can be a very rewarding drive and the road follows the course of the river through mopane and thick riverine bush in places; leopards are often seen here. Once you reach the H1-6, either retrace your steps or take the tar road north heading back to camp.

The Northern Region

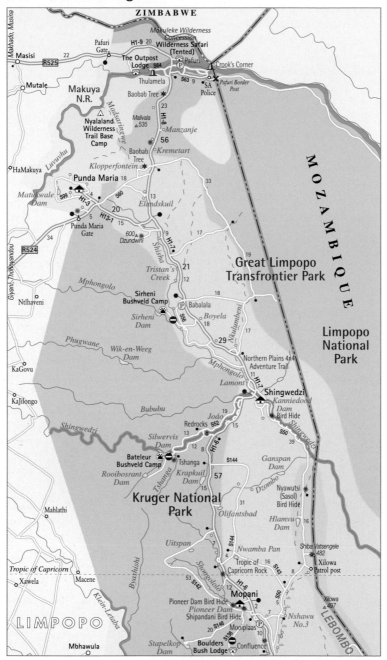

Mopani
Northern Region

Overlooking the Pioneer Dam, on an attractive hillside dotted with baobabs, Mopani Rest Camp, with its thatched, square, face-brick 'houses', is a significant departure from the traditional rondawel architecture of the park. This large camp has a quiet, peaceful atmosphere. The surrounding mopane shrubveld does not yield that many game sightings and, at times, it feels as if even the animals are taking a break.

Left: Accommodation units at Mopani are modern and comfortable. Above: The bar and restaurant overlook the Pioneer Dam and often provide great sightings over a gin and tonic.

Accommodation

Chalets Mopani offers four-bed bungalows and four bed cottages, both with fully equipped kitchenette and bathroom. Also available are six-bed family cottages with three twin rooms, one en-suite bathroom and two other bathrooms and a full kitchen. Xanatseni Guest House sleeps eight and has a lounge/dining room, kitchen, outside covered bar and a braai.

Tsendze Rustic Campsite recently opened some 8 km south of Mopani near Mooiplas picnic area (book at Mopani). The main rest camp also has a large, hi-tech conference centre.

Wildlife

The camp A large baobab grows in camp and an in-camp trail winds through the interesting landscape, allowing you to get some exercise and providing a good opportunity to see a diverse array of birds, especially in the summer months, and giant plated lizards (males with red heads). Look out for water birds, not to mention crocodile and hippo on the dam. From the lady's bar, waterbuck, impala, warthog, elephant and buffalo can even be seen drinking on occasion.

The surroundings Tsessebe, roan and eland are all occasionally seen in the region. Caracal and black-backed jackal are seen relatively often.

The Big Five Lion sightings are infrequent and rhino are seldom spotted in the area. Leopard, however, are common and large numbers of buffalo and elephant occur here.

Birds Keep an eye out for mosque swallows in the baobabs and wire-

Visitors can overnight in the Shipandani Bird Hide. It sleeps up to six, and there are mosquito shutters and folded beds. Book at reception at Mopani.

Midday is bad for game viewing but great for swimming — remember to use sunblock!

tailed swallows in camp. An interesting collection of water birds gathers at Pioneer Dam, in particular painted snipe, osprey and African fish eagle. Kittlitz's plover, chestnut-backed sparrowlark and collared (red-winged) pratincole can all be seen too.

Don't miss!

The in-camp trail is a must before heading to the bar for sundowners on the deck overlooking Pioneer Dam. Yet another highlight is the extremely rewarding game-viewing offered by the relatively out-of-the-way **Stapelkop**

MOPANI REST CAMP

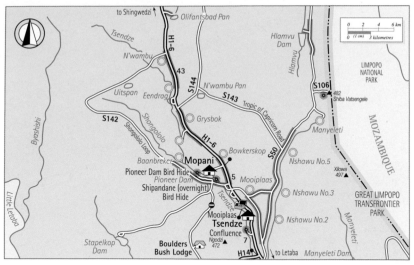

Dam, which boasts plenty of good vantage points and welcome tranquillity.

Activities

Morning, sunset and night drives and morning and afternoon walks may all be booked at reception. Wildlife documentaries are shown in the open-air theatre when weather permits.

Best drives

Even though game-viewing can be a little frustrating from Mopani, the relatively large network of roads surrounding the camp makes it easy to avoid the traffic jams associated with good sightings in the southern parts of the park. Here, as you amble along the mopane-lined dirt roads, you can truly feel as if you have the place to yourself.

Nshawu/Tropic of Capricorn Loop
This is the most 'productive' route in the region. To get there, take the short access road from Mopani back to the

tarred H1-6 (the Letaba–Shingwedzi Road), turning south and continuing along until you reach the S49 dirt road to your left. Here you pass a number of research plots where the effects of different fire regimes on the mopane ecosystem are being tested. Birders should look out for 'scorched-earth specialists' such as Kittlitz's plover, red-capped lark and Temminck's courser.

You have two options: about 3 km after you leave the tar, the road turns left, heading past the **Mooiplaas Water Hole** and then onto the S50 (Nshawu Vlei–Dipene Road). Roan have been released into this area; also look out for eland. Alternatively, continue straight on the S49 for another 8 km until you reach the S50 Nshawu Road and only then do you turn left. This option adds 16 km to the route but includes three more water holes **Nshawu One, Two** and **Three**.

Heading north along the S50, it is

worth taking the short side track down to the **Nshawu Dam** (damaged in the floods of 2000). This is situated in an open grassy area, so game-viewing is good. The dam itself attracts elephant, particularly in the late afternoon when they come down to drink, and also provides a good opportunity to see hippo, crocodile and water birds, such as comb (knob-billed) duck, moorhen, Kittlitz's plover, African spoonbill, blacksmith lapwing and, occasionally, saddle-billed stork. Look out for tsessebe in the grassy areas around the dam, plus the many grassland birds that occur here, including Swainson's and Natal spurfowl, Shelley's francolin, red-crested korhaan, black-bellied and kori bustard, crowned lapwing and Montagu's harrier.

Further along the S50, take the left-hand turn-off onto the S143 (**Tropic of Capricorn Loop**), which passes through patches of open grassland

Above and top: Mopani is a large camp overlooking the Pioneer Dam in the northern regions of the park.

between dense mopane stands, where you are likely to see giraffe, zebra and elephant. Turn left when you reach the S144, which takes you back to the H1-6 tar road through a small gabbro intrusion covered with thornveld.

Back at the H1-6, turn left (or south) towards Mopani, but resist the temptation to speed up as you head for home because good sightings are often seen at **Grysbok** and **Bowker's Kop water holes**. In particular, keep a lookout here for sable, especially in the area around Bowker's Kop. The H1-6 also crosses the Tropic of Capricorn a few kilometres after you rejoin the tar, where a small plaque indicates the spot.

Shongololo Loop The first few kilometres of the southern section of this loop (which follows the S142) can be very rewarding as it skirts the **Pioneer Dam** and thus attracts a variety of animals, including elephant, waterbuck, warthog, impala and others. It is also worth stopping a while at the

Shipandani Hide, which overlooks the dam, providing you with a comfortable seat from which to view the birdlife, notably pied kingfisher hunting from nearby branches or hovering over water, African spoonbill, red-billed teal, and both white-breasted and reed cormorant. Continuing along, the route remains productive up until **Baanbreker Water Hole**, but after that, the thick mopane offers little in the way of good sightings. However, you can never really tell what animal will be sitting in the road ahead....

Once you reach the H1-6 (Letaba–Shingwedzi Road) head south, keeping a lookout along the way as the road passes through a small gabbro intrusion so the vegetation changes briefly to thornveld, before reverting to tall mopane veld and shrub mopane. Watch for sable all along the route, especially near the **Bowker's Kop Water Hole**.

Stapelkop Dam Many people are put off by the 18 km drive down the S146 (Stapelkop Dam Road), so those who make the journey often have the place to themselves. There are a number of good vantage points over the dam and this allows visitors good views of hippo, crocodile and numerous water birds, including African jacana, hamerkop, green-backed and squacco heron, dwarf bittern, red-billed teal and comb (knob-billed) and white-faced duck.

Having made the journey, it is well worth spending a few hours in a good spot watching the comings and goings of the birds and game animals.

Tsendze Loop Although this loop is a little far from Mopani, if you have

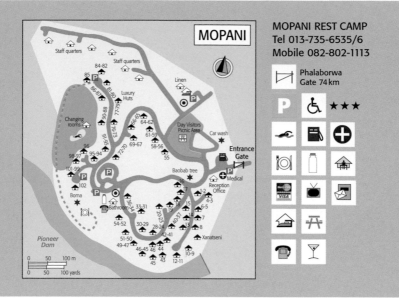

MOPANI

MOPANI REST CAMP
Tel 013-735-6535/6
Mobile 082-802-1113

Phalaborwa
Gate 74 km

Staff quarters

Staff quarters

84-82

85

86-59

88-86

Luxury Huts

Changing rooms

74-73

95-94

96

98-97

101-99

102

Boma

Linen

Day Visitors Picnic Area

Car wash

Entrance Gate

Baobab tree

Medical

Reception Office

Bathroom

54-52

30-29

33-31

51-50

49-47

46-45

45

43

12-11

10-9

Xanatseni

Pioneer Dam

0   50   100 m
0   50   100 yards

had little luck with sightings it is worth the drive, as this route often offers pleasant surprises. Leopard are often seen along the road. Head south on the H1-6, past the turn-offs to the S49, S50 and H14, and turning right on the S48 Tsendze Loop shortly after the Nshawu River. The road runs along the Tsendze River through a mixture of mopane, mahogany, sycamore figs and other large trees that line the water course, before returning to the H1-6 tar road after about 17 km. Turn left here and head north.

You can take the S50 Nshawu Road if you want to delay your arrival back home and complete the **Tropic of Capricorn Loop** described earlier. There is a relatively new sleepover hide on the Tsendze River, which boasts nine beds that fold down from the walls, as well as a fenced-in braai area

The Tropic of Capricorn is well marked north of Mopani.

and toilets. Another hide has been built on the **Pioneer Dam**, allowing a different perspective of a familiar spot.

Bateleur
Bush Camp
Northern Region

The sign – "Welcome to the smallest, oldest and friendliest of bush camps" – says it all. Tucked away in attractive countryside along the Red Rocks Road southwest of Shingwedzi, this attractive camp, built in the 1980s, allows you to escape main-line Kruger. There is a good hide in camp overlooking a small water hole. Two large dams – Silwervis and Rooibosrant, located close to camp – ensure that game is good.

Above: The camp is well shaded by spreading trees. Below: There is an excellent hide in camp overlooking a small water hole.

Accommodation

Chalets There are four- and six-bed, fully equipped guest cottages, all of which have televisions. The cottages are separated by magnificent sycamore figs and have comfortable stoeps, allowing you to relax in peace after the hard day's game viewing. Conference facilities are available, if you need to mix a little work with your pleasure.

Wildlife

The camp Pearl-spotted and African scops owl frequent the trees and a collection of interesting birds and wildlife can be seen drinking at the water hole from the hide in camp.

The surroundings Both nearby dams are worth visiting as impala, waterbuck and, occasionally, elephant congregate around these, especially in the dry winter months. Leopards are commonly spotted in the Red Rocks area. Rhino are occasionally spotted along the S52 after the **Red Rocks Water Hole**. There are also magnificent views from the Tshanga Viewpoint where you can stretch your legs.

The Big Five Rhino and lion are scarce, but elephant, buffalo and leopard all occur in the region.

Birds The impressive trees in camp host a variety of interesting birds, including little banded goshawk, but the real treat for keen birders is the water birds on the surrounding dams and water holes. Most notable of these are African spoonbill, fish eagle, comb (knob-billed) duck, red-billed teal, hamerkop, greenshank, marsh, wood and common sandpiper, little stint and, occasionally, greater painted snipe.

MOPANE TREES

The landscape of Kruger north of the Olifants River is dominated by mopane trees (*Colophospermum mopane*). They are rounded trees generally 5–12m in height, although larger individuals up to 22m occur occasionally. They are easily recognised by their green, butterfly-shaped leaves after which the trees are named – *mopane* means 'butterfly' in Venda. Traditionally, people utilise the twigs to clean their teeth; chewed leaves are applied to wounds; and infused bark is used for diarrhoea. Most importantly, however, the larvae of the mopane emperor moth (*Gonimbrasia belina*), feed exclusively on mopane leaves in the summer, and are eaten throughout the region, providing an excellent source of protein for humans and other animals.

Don't miss!

Spending a lazy lunchtime at **Tshanga Viewpoint** overlooking miles of mopane and bushwillow woodlands.

Activities

Morning and sunset drives, as well as morning and afternoon walks, are booked at reception.

BATELEUR BUSH CAMP

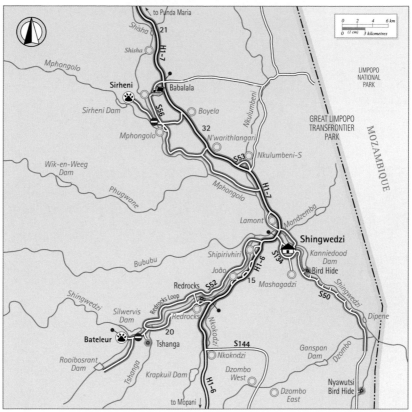

Best drives

Silwervis Dam This dam is well populated with hippo and crocodile but, unfortunately, the vegetation is relatively thick so views over the dam are limited. If you get there early in the morning, you are likely to encounter hippos still out grazing at the water.

Rooibosrant Dam The vegetation around this dam is less thick and the roads are positioned close to the water, allowing for good sightings and photography. This is especially true in the wet season when the dam is full.

The dam itself is a relatively large and attractive body of water studded with dead trees that play host to a number of birds. Numerous animals congregate here to drink and you are certain to see waterbuck, crocodile and hippo. The view from the road faces west so this makes a good morning photography spot, with warm light falling on your subjects. At sunset you will get interesting silhouettes and reflections in the water from the trees, although remember to leave enough time to get back to camp before the gates close.

22 Shingwedzi
Northern Region

Shingwedzi is a medium-sized camp deep in the heart of the mopane shrubveld in the northeast of the park. The surroundings are thickly vegetated and game-viewing in the area can prove frustrating. Having said that, the camp itself is near the Kanniedood Dam on the Shingwedzi River. In the dry season, this usually teems with wildlife, including large herds of elephant, congregating at this reliable water source.

If you're camping at Shingwedzi, get in early to grab a spot in the shade.

Accommodation

Chalets Three-bed huts utilise communal ablutions and kitchens, while the two- and five-bed (two beds in a loft) bungalows have full kitchenettes as well as bathrooms. Certain of the two-bed units have double beds. Four-person cottages and the Rentmeester Guesthouse sleeps eight. It has, mercifully in summer, a swimming pool. When built, the main building boasted the world's largest thatch roof. The camp units have been extensively upgraded. A day centre is planned.

Camping and caravanning Shingwedzi is essentially a large sandy area with no allocated sites and relatively limited shade is available, so get in early to claim a good spot. Standard caravan-plug electrical boxes are scattered throughout the area. It is well served by large ablutions and two communal kitchens.

Wildlife

The camp Look out for palm swifts that live in the tall palm trees near reception. In addition, elephant and other game regularly drink at the river, which is clearly visible from the deck outside the restaurant.

The surroundings Be on the alert for a large bull elephant called Tshilonde. Sharpe's grysbok are also sometimes seen in the riverine areas near camp, while tree monitors can be found in the larger trees. Verreaux's (giant) eagle owl are common in the trees lining the road into camp. The north of Shingwedzi, in the Babalala area, is a good place to see roan, sable, tsessebe, eland and Lichtenstein's hartebeest. Kudu, bushbuck, nyala, waterbuck and spotted

All rest-camp units in Kruger (except the tents) are air conditioned, which is great for hot summer nights! It means you can keep cool while keeping your room mosquito – and malaria – free.

hyena are common, while wild dog are regulars, if endangered.

The Big Five Rhino were introduced into the region and can be spotted although they are less common than further south. A large lion pride is always in the area – generally following the large buffalo herds that occur in the region. Elephant are very common, while leopard are often seen in the riverine areas.

Birds If you take a seat at the restaurant or in the picnic area overlooking the river, you will see both red-billed and southern yellow-billed hornbill, African mourning dove, and grey go-away-bird (lourie). Keep a look out for these interesting specials in the surroundings: Bennett's woodpecker, European hobby, bat hawk, broad-billed roller, and mosque swallow. Arnot's chat will be found in the mopane woodland surrounding the camp, which is also known for its owls, including Verreaux's (giant) eagle owl in the trees lining the road into camp.

Don't miss!

The large matriarchal herds of elephant are fascinating, so spend some time observing the constant interactions between individuals in these close-knit family units ... also the restaurant serves the best steak in Kruger!

Activities

Morning, sunset and night drives, as well as guided morning and afternoon bushwalks may all be booked at reception. Wildlife documentaries are shown, weather permitting.

Best drives

A number of good routes radiate out from Shingwedzi. The proximity of water and the associated thick riverine vegetation makes this one of the most productive areas for game-viewing in the north of the park.

Kanniedood Dam Take the S50 (Nshawe Vlei–Dipene Road) south from camp, which follows the banks of the Kanniedood Dam for the first couple of kilometres and then continues along the course of the Shingwedzi River. A number of turn-offs allow you to get relatively close to the dam, providing you with excellent sightings of hippo and crocodile, while elephant are abundant and are often seen cooling off in the hot weather by swimming or spraying themselves with water. The area is also fantastic for birdlife and many water birds, including the rare saddle-billed stork, are found at the water's edge. A small hide has been built overlooking the dam and is worth visiting, although the turn-offs to the dam itself actually offer you a greater variety and, in many cases, a better view. The dam attracts white-winged and whiskered tern, black-winged stilt, collared (red-winged) pratincole, greater painted snipe, and waders such as curlew and common sandpiper (in summer). Also look for lesser jacana, pygmy goose,

Day visitors at Shingwedzi are welcome to braai or join camp residents at the camp restaurant ... which, incidentally, serves the best steak in Kruger!

glossy ibis, comb (knob-billed) and white-faced duck. Thick-billed weavers nest at the water's edge.

If you continue along the S50, you pass the attractive **Nyawutsi Hide**, which overlooks a rocky pool offering a good opportunity to see terrapins and water birds rather close. Yellow-billed stork and little egret can be seen fishing in the shallows along the edge. Eventually, after 52 km, you will reach the right-hand turn-off to the S143

Visitors are treated to the spectacular river scenery as they cross the low-level bridge near camp on their way home from a guided game drive.

(**The Tropic of Capricorn Loop**), which takes you back to the tar H1-6 heading back to camp. This is a relatively long drive, however, so it may be a better idea to turn around and retrace your steps, back along the S50, once you feel you've covered enough ground.

Red Rocks This attractive route follows a rocky, steep-sided valley to the west of Shingwedzi Rest Camp and offers the possibility of some great sightings in very attractive settings. Take the tar road west from camp, keeping a lookout for the resident leopard that often frequents this stretch, and then turn left at the T-junction with the H1-6, following this for 3 km before turning right onto the S52 (**Shingwedzi North Loop**) on Red Rocks Route. Most people agree that the northern part of the loop is the most attractive and productive, so drive this first. Keep a sharp lookout in the open pan-like areas as

rhino are often spotted here, and these can be very difficult to spot elsewhere in the north. The road is renowned for leopard and lion sightings, especially on the rocks where they sun themselves in the morning. The tiny Sharpe's grysbok also occurs along this stretch.

A number of viewpoints offer superb views over the river in a deep-cut valley below, and it is well worth getting out at the **Red Rocks Viewpoint** and stretching your legs while you take in the attractive scenery. If you wish to make a day of it, pack a picnic lunch and head out to **Tshanga Viewpoint** where you can enjoy your lunch overlooking a vista of mixed thornveld that grows on a small gabbro intrusion in the area. The picnic site is not serviced and has a simple long-drop toilet and a few tables, but it is peaceful as not many people stop here, preferring to return to Shingwedzi and a fry-up brunch.

SHINGWEDZI

Entrance Gate
Bathroom
Medical
Reception
Office
Rentmeester
Bathroom
Kitchen
49-45 44-40
Kitchen
56-58
59-61
B
Bathroom
62-64
65-67 68-69
Kitchen
17-21 22-26
Kitchen
Tap in the tree
A
Conference Centre
Housekeeping
Entrance Gate
30-31
Staff quarters

0   50   100 m
0   50   100 yards

SHINGWEDZI REST CAMP
Tel 013-735-6806/7
Mobile 082-889-4376

Punda Maria
Gate 72 km

★★★

Fuel is available here, as at most of the larger camps in Kruger.

Mphongolo Loop A very worthwhile drive is the S56, the northern road that follows the Mphongolo River. Again, head west from Shingwedzi, turning right at the T-junction with the tarred H1-6. When crossing the bridge over the Shingwedzi, keep a watch out for wildlife – from mongoose and baboon to kudu, leopard and elephant – moving along the dry river course. Continue, taking the S55 dirt-road loop past **Lamont Water Hole**. This rejoins the tar just 3 km further on. Continue on the H1-7 for another 4 km before turning left onto the S56, the Mphongolo Loop. This road threads its way through the majestic riverine forest passing under immense jackalberry, sycamore fig and tamboti trees. There are numerous turn-offs to the river and it is well worth taking each one as animal life can be prolific along here, especially baboon, bushbuck, waterbuck and, very often, leopard. Even if there are no animals, birdlife along this stretch is busy and it would be criminal not to tackle it with your binoculars and bird book within easy reach. Be on the lookout for African green pigeon, cuckoos, woodland kingfisher and many of the typical forest species that sometimes occur in these dense riverine forests, such as blue-mantled flycatcher and trumpeter hornbill. Make sure you return home with enough time to enjoy sunset from the high-water bridge.

Sirheni Bush Camp
Northern Region

23

This pretty bushveld camp, tucked away on a corner of the Mphongolo River overlooking the Sirheni Dam, is another of my favourite places in Kruger. The name is derived from the Shangaan word for 'cemetery' and refers to a collection of elephant skeletons that were found nearby. All the cottages look out onto the dam and, from the comfort of your deckchair, you are likely to see an array of animals, including hippo in the water and waterbuck, warthog, impala and occasionally elephant drinking. In addition, there are plenty of interesting animal sightings to be had in the surroundings.

Sirheni Bush Camp is tucked away, overlooking the Sirheni Dam, which attracts a plethora of wildife; you can often watch elephants from your cottage.

Accommodation

Chalets There are four-bed cottages with two beds in one room and two bench beds in the lounge, as well as six-bed cottages, available at Sirheni. All units have fully equipped kitchenettes and bathrooms.

Wildlife

The camp A wide range of animals drink at the dam and can be seen from your room or the hide. Most notable of these are elephant, waterbuck, impala and warthog.

The surroundings Eland, roan, sable, tsessebe, Lichtenstein's hartebeest and reedbuck can all be seen in the surrounding open grasslands, while Sharpe's grysbok are often seen in riverine areas. Cheetah are regularly seen on the H1-7 (Shingwedzi–Punda Maria Road), near the Babalala Picnic Site. African wild cat and serval also feature near the camp.

The Big Five Rhino are difficult to find, but elephant and buffalo are common, and lion tend to occur near the buffalo herds. Leopard are common in the densely vegetated riverine areas along the Mphongolo Loop.

Birds A number of water birds congregate on the Sirheni Dam: look out for rufous-bellied heron, dwarf bittern, whiskered tern, African pygmy goose and greater painted snipe.

Don't miss!

This is a fantastic camp from which to launch your quest to see some of the rarer antelope in the park – good luck in finding roan, sable, tsessebe, Lichtenstein's hartebeest and Sharpe's grysbok.

The Mphongolo Loop in the mopane belt is a great place to spot Arnot's chat.

The camp hide often offers up a surprising array of sightings. However, you won't struggle to find Swainson's spurfowl (opposite top) or tree squirrels (opposite botttom).

Activities

Morning, sunset and night drives and morning and afternoon walks are all booked at reception.

Best drives

The great thing about staying at Sirheni is that you can access the northern parts of the excellent **Mphongolo Loop** before the masses from Shingwedzi arrive! Follow the private access road from the camp joining the S56, a dirt road that forms the Mphongolo Loop, at the cross roads. If you go north (left) towards **Babalala Picnic Site**, the road continues for 8km before joining the H1-7 (Shingwedzi–Punda Road). Look out for cheetah along this section and along the H1-7 once you reach it. If you turn south (right) off the S56, the road winds through typical mixed mopane/bushwillow woodlands along the Mphongolo Stream, before it joins the Phugwane River lined with thick riverine vegetation. All along this road, keep a lookout for leopard as this thick riverine habitat is prime territory for them.

Sirheni Bushveld Camp is well situated for longer drives to the Pafuri Region and Crooks Corner (see 'Best drives' in Punda Maria). This is a full day's outing, however, so take a picnic lunch and stop over at the beautiful **Pafuri Picnic Site**. You can also head south to the scenic **Red Rocks** area (see 'Best drives' in Shingwedzi on page 126). Again it is advisable to make a full day's outing of this trip, taking a picnic lunch that could be enjoyed at **Tshanga Picnic Site**. This peaceful spot has no services other than a long-drop toilet and a few tables and benches; it is better to walk up the short path and find a spot on the rocks overlooking the surroundings.

24 Punda Maria
Northern Region

This quaint rest camp at the foot of the pretty Gumbandebvu Hill is the northernmost SANParks camp in Kruger. As such, it provides a convenient base from which to explore the bird-rich Luvuvhu Valley, botanically diverse sandveld and magnificent archaeological ruins of the ancient citadel of Thulamela. Captain JJ Coetser, the first ranger, named the camp Punda Maria after his wife Maria, who it is said, was fond of wearing striped dresses – Punda Maria being a play on the Swahili for zebra, *punda maliya*. The camp is shady and peaceful and, although extensively upgraded (swimming pool, waterhole and hide, new gate complex and day centre), contains much of its sought-after rough-hewn leadwood 1920s feel.

Punda Maria was named after zebras.

Accommodation

Chalets Two-bed bungalows, with en-suite bathrooms, utilise communal kitchen facilities, although they are equipped with fridges. Three-bed bungalows with both bathrooms and kitchens are also available. The two family cottages sleep four people each – two beds in the bedroom and two in the lounge – and have a small kitchenette and bathroom. These have private braai facilities, but the bungalows use communal braais. A small swimming pool has recently been added.

Safari tents There are seven luxury, four-person, permanent safari tents. These have en-suite bathrooms and fully equipped kitchenettes.

Camping and caravanning There is a large camp site with communal kitchens that have two-plate electric stoves, washing facilities and instant hot-water dispensers. Electrical points with caravan sockets are scattered throughout, but these are limited, so you need to indicate whether you require power when booking.

Wildlife

The camp Elephant shrews often dash about the camp at night, while numerous owls frequent the trees, filling the night with their calls.

The surroundings The camp is located in the delicate sandveld vegetation and is one of the best places to see the rare Sharpe's grysbok. Zebra, buffalo, kudu and nyala are common in the area, while eland, sable and wild dogs are seen regularly. Before the devastating drought of the 1990s, nyala were extremely common, but their numbers were decimated, and are only no[w] the increase. Wild dog in partic[ular] are often spotted in the early mornin[g]. (See also 'Best drives' on page 134.)

The Big Five You will battle to find rhino this far north and lion can be hard to find too. Leopard are seen regularly, however, especially on the loop roads around the camp. Elephant and buffalo are also common.

Birds A number of specials – including crested guineafowl and Pel's fishing owl (resting up in large riverine trees during the day) – occur in the region, particularly along the Luvuvhu Valley. The best birding is unquestionably during the summer months, when many migrants, such as carmine bee-eater, icterine, marsh, olive-tree and river warbler, broad-billed roller and cuckoos return. Raptors are more numerous at this time of year too. Steppe, lesser-spotted and Wahlberg's eagle, steppe buzzard, black (yellow-billed) kite and Eurasian hobby may be seen in summer. In winter, a pair of African hawk eagles breed on the hill behind the camp. In the evening, large numbers of vultures and marabou storks roost outside the camp gates.

Don't miss!

The five-hour tour to Thulamela (see page 179). This majestic site commands an impressive view of the surroundings and offers a fascinating glimpse

the Iron Age cultures that flourished in the area.

Also, don't miss the **Paradise Flycatcher Nature Trail** through camp, which provides a great excuse to stretch your legs and take in some of the spectacular birdlife that flocks to the northern reaches of the park, particularly during the summer months. Look for yellow-bellied greenbul, white-bellied sunbird, African paradise, blue-grey and grey tit (fan-tailed) flycatcher, and orange-breasted bush-shrike. Some of the best birding can be done at the bird bath on the outer wall opposite the picnic area. Also keep an eye open for the magnificent leopard orchid in the trunk of a dead leadwood being choked by a strangler fig right outside the main office/restaurant.

Activities

Guided tours to **Thulamela** leave in the morning and last about five hours. Morning, sunset and night drives are also available. Regular guided bushwalks are not offered, although walks for four or more people can be arranged if done well in advance.

Best drives

Situated in the ecologically diverse sandveld ecozone, Punda Maria is surrounded by a wide and interesting array of plant life, which differs from the monospecific stands of mopane common to the tree mopane savanna and mopane shrubveld along the H13-1 (Punda Gate Road), H1-7 (Shingwedzi–Punda Road) and H1-8.

Mahonie Loop This attractive route winds through diverse sandveld com-

BAOBABS

The San believed there were no young baobabs (*Adansonia digitata*) but that the gods – for whatever reason – simply planted the adult trees upside down. What is more, they believed that a lion would kill anyone who picked the white flowers that appear in the evening (and fall the next morning) between October and December.

Baobab wood is light and useless, although people have traditionally used the bark to make rope. The leaves are eaten as a vegetable. In addition the leaves, bark and the white pulp of the fruit, which contains tartaric acid, are used to relieve fevers and treat diarrhoea.

munities dotted with large termite mounds. These slopes are heavily wooded with tree species such as the silver clusterleaf, various bushwillows, pod mahoganies and white syringa. Look out for buffalo, kudu and nyala (which are quite common) along the way. Sharpe's grysbok and suni (both rare, shy and tiny antelope species) are also sometimes seen along this route. A pack of wild dog frequents this area, lion are sometimes seen in the area,

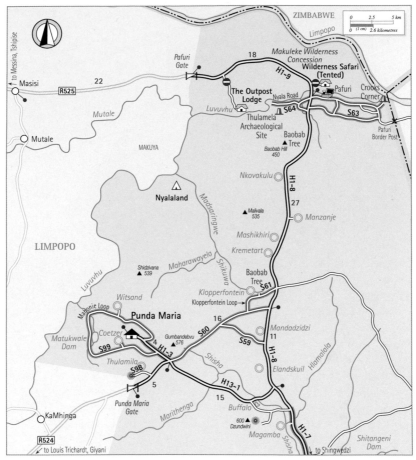

while leopard are seen fairly frequently towards the evening. Along the route, stop off at the **Witsand Water Hole**, which offers some good viewing and is conveniently situated for photographers as you are able to stay until evening light and still make it back to camp before the gates close.

Thulamila Viewpoint Do not confuse **Thulamila**, south of the camp, with the **Thulamela Archaeological Site** in the far north, which can be accessed only on a guided walk (bookings at Punda Maria). Thulamila provides a fantastic view over the northern parts of the park, but the road leading up to it is very rough and you will need a tough or off-road vehicle.

Dzundzwini Viewpoint To get to Dzundzwini, take the H13-1 south towards Shingwedzi, which passes through sandveld before changing to tree mopane savanna after a couple of kilometres, and then the right-hand

Above: These magical stones guard Thulamela. Left: Nyala are most common in the north.

turn onto the S58 dirt road. The road passes a plaque under a large sausage tree on the left, a kilometre or so before the turn to **Dzundzwini**, which marks the temporary camp site of ranger JJ Coetser – the founder of Punda Maria – before he moved to permanent quarters at Punda Maria in 1919. Turn right and follow the road as it winds up to the viewpoint, which looks south over the flat mopane-carpeted landscape.

Klopperfontein Dam Follow the H13-2 out of Punda Maria, turning left onto the S60 about 3 km from the gate and follow this dirt road north as it traverses through sandveld and then enters tree-mopane savanna. The route is quite open and has good grazing so relatively good animal sightings are possible. In particular look out for sable as you approach Klopperfontein Dam, which contains resident crocodiles and an assortment of water birds. In summer, look for the elusive corn crake in the surrounding grasslands. The dam

A baobab tree with a 5 m radius is approximately 1 000 years old.

was named after Dirk Klopper, an ivory hunter of the late 1800s.

Pafuri/Crook's Corner This area is a must for any visitor to the north of the park. It is a full day's outing from Punda Maria, but the excellent **Pafuri Picnic Site** is an awesome spot at which to stop for lunch. Take the H13-2 out of camp, turning onto the S60 and follow this all the way to the H1-8, heading north. The tar road passes through relatively thick mopane shrubveld and sightings are difficult to come by, but keep an eye out for nyala and kudu, which sometimes feed close to the road. In open areas, you may spot eland along this road. This area is also the only place in the park to see crested guineafowl and African finfoot. The picnic site is the place to see wattle-eyed flycatcher, tropical boubou, gorgeous bushshrike, white-browed (Heuglin's) robin-chat

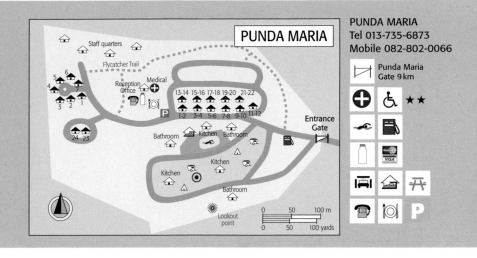

PUNDA MARIA
Tel 013-735-6873
Mobile 082-802-0066

and yellow white-eye. Also look out for Pel's fishing owl.

About 16 km from where you joined the H1-8, look out for **Baobab Hill** to the west. This used to be the first outspan or camp site (a plaque marks the spot) for migrant workers from the northern areas (what is now Mozambique), who had been recruited to work in the gold mines of the interior. After Baobab Hill, the road dips into the Luvuvhu River flood plain and the vegetation becomes thicker and more varied.

Do not take the S63, the first tar road to the right, as this is a relatively boring run up to the border post; rather continue for another 2 km to the dirt road (also the S63) running along the Luvuvhu River. It is well worth continuing past this turn-off and continuing on to the bridge over the Luvuvhu – a few hundred metres further. Actually stop on the bridge for a few minutes because a tremendous amount of life pulses through the lush riverine bush

lining the river. In particular, keep a sharp lookout for Sharpe's grysbok, suni, samango monkeys (which you will not see anywhere else in the park other than along the Luvuvhu River) and birds such as African finfoot, white-fronted plover, Pel's fishing owl and crested guineafowl. Nyala, vervet monkeys and baboons are common in this region.

Turn back and head towards **Crook's Corner**, passing the picnic spot, and follow the course of the Luvuvhu as it winds its way through the lush flood plain. The road passes under stately fig trees, jackalberries and a forest of fever trees. Take every turn-off to the river and keep a lookout as many bird and animal species that are really difficult to spot elsewhere occur here. You could see kudu and nyala, baboons and monkeys (including samango) and, in the summer, the area is full of rarely seen bird species, such as broad-billed and racket-tailed roller, icterine and river warbler and thrush nightingale.

25 Private concessions and lodges

During a rationalisation process in the 1990s, SANParks realised that certain under-utilised areas of Kruger could be developed, with care, to increase tourism revenues. The best approach, it was decided, was to offer them to private enterprises for up-market lodge development. This ensured maximum financial benefits with minimal environmental impact – the theory being that 12 high-paying guests would have less impact than 120 guests paying SAN-Parks rates ... or something to that effect. These private concessions have also diversified Kruger's clientele, allowing SANParks to compete on level terms with the luxurious lodges of the various private reserves outside its borders. So far, the strategy has proved successful; the park monitors all the activities of the concessionaires, ensuring the lodges have minimal impact on the environment, while the leasing of concession rights and revenues earned have already realised handsome returns. There are eight concessions with 17 luxurious private lodges currently operational within Kruger National Park

Whether you're looking for a health breakfast or cigars and Champagne, you'll not be disappointed in the new ultra-luxurious private lodges in Kruger.

PAFURI CAMP
(MAKULEKE CONCESSION)

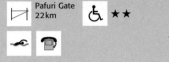

PAFURI CAMP
Tel 011-257-5111, Fax 011-807-2110
E-mail: info@safariadventure.co.za
Website: www.wilderness-safaris.com

Pafuri Gate
22 km ♿ ★★

This Wilderness Safaris luxury tented camp is situated on the northern bank of the Luvuvhu River within the vast 24 000 ha Makuleke concession, in the far northern region of Kruger. As such, it offers discerning visitors a fantastic opportunity to explore this ecologically diverse and archaeologically rich region of the Kruger National Park. Partnerships between tourist lodges and communities, such as this one between Wilderness Safaris and the Makuleke, are proving successful and, indeed, are viewed by many as a 'textbook' example of how local communities and conservation initiatives can coexist successfully.

Accommodation

This child-friendly camp has 20 tented rooms with six family rooms for up to four people. The camp is divided into a seven-tent Pafuri East and 13-tent Pafuri West, each with its own plunge pool, deck and boma. The tents are simple yet stylishly decorated with a Makuleke influence, and raised on wooden platforms 2 m off the ground. All have electric lighting, a ceiling fan and en-suite bathrooms. The communal dining and bar area lies nestled at

the feet of the gigantic jackalberry trees, which shade the camp against the sun's fierce onslaught.

Wildlife

The camp Situated in lush riverine vegetation on the banks of the Luvuvhu River, Pafuri camp offers great views of a variety of game including elephant and nyala as they come to drink. Birdlife is prolific and a Pel's fishing owl has been known to roost in camp. At night the riparian forest is alive with the calls of African scops and barred owls, as well as Verreaux's (giant) eagle owl.

The surroundings Although plains game, such as zebra and wildebeest, occurs at lower densities than in central Kruger, along the Luvuvhu River you are almost guaranteed sightings of elephant and buffalo that frequent the

Pafuri's comfortable tented camp (top) is located on the banks of the Luvuvhu (above).

region year round. The dense riverine vegetation harbours nyala, impala and kudu, while you have excellent opportunities to see Sharpe's grysbok and, if you're lucky, eland. Both wild dog and cheetah have been seen nearby. The Pafuri region is also renowned as one of the best birding destinations in South Africa, offering visitors the chance of seeing a variety of rarely seen species.

The Big Five In a joint venture between Wilderness Safaris and the Kruger National Park, white rhino have been re-introduced into the area and all members of the Big Five may be seen here. Lion can be difficult to spot in the area, although a resident pride does frequent the lodge area. Leopard thrive in the riverine vegetation and large herds of both elephant and buffalo often lead to impressive sightings.

Birds Crested guineafowl, white-crowned lapwing, Pel's fishing owl, Böhm's and mottled spinetail, tropical boubou, narina trogon, black-throated wattle-eye, orange-winged (golden-backed) pytilia, crowned eagle, racket-tailed roller and Retz's (red-billed) helmetshrike occur in the region.

Don't miss!

Even though this luxury tented lodge is located in one of the warmest regions in the park, do not let the opportunity of undertaking guided walks pass you by as these are an excellent way to see a variety of skittish species often spooked by vehicles. If walking is not for you, make sure you book brunch at the spectacular **Lanner Gorge** – a wonderful six-to-eight-hour guided trip not to be missed.

Activities

Game drives in open 4x4s, night drives, guided bushwalks and sleep-out hides are available. Guided trips to **Thulamela Archaeological Site** should not be missed. Recent additions are a **Makuleke Village** homestay and a wilderness walking trail (three or four nights).

THE OUTPOST (MAKULEKE CONCESSION)

THE OUTPOST
Tel 011-245-5704/086-636-5364
E-mail: sue@klpg.co.za
Website: www.theoutpost.co.za

Pafuri Gate 15 km   ★★★

Mini bar

This was the first luxury lodge (bold glass, steel and timber) erected on the Makuleke Concession in the very far north of the park, some 15 km from the Pafuri Gate. The concession is owned by the Makuleke people, removed to facilitate expansion of the park in 1969. After a successful land claim case in the 1990s, the land reverted to its rightful owners. The Makuleke have decided to continue managing the area for conservation and have formed various partnerships in order to build luxury lodges on the concession.

Accommodation

The lodge accommodates 24 people in 12 angular, ultra-modern (and award-winning), stylish living 'spaces' strung along a prominent hillside that provides magnificent views over the Luvuvhu

The Outpost has a commanding view over the Luvuvhu River Valley.

River Valley. Each 'space' has only two permanent walls – the other two are removable – which allows tremendous privacy, while offering a sweeping vista from the air-conditioned comfort of your suite.

This open design runs throughout the lodge and wherever you find yourself – whether enjoying a cocktail in the bar, lounging on one of the trendy couches in the communal lounge or relaxing in the pool after a hard morning of game-viewing – wild Africa seems to peer over your shoulder.

Wildlife

The camp From your room, there are magnificent views over the confluence of the Luvuvhu and Mutale rivers and herds of antelope and elephants are a common sight as they come to drink. Leopard are regularly heard around camp and occasionally seen prowling in the vicinity. Buffalo are common.

The surroundings This far north, wildlife is harder to find, although guests are able to see a selection of animals rarely seen further south, such as Sharpe's grysbok, samango monkeys and nyala. Birdlife in the area is prolific and the region has to be one of the best birding destinations in the country. Rare species such as crested guineafowl and Pel's fishing owl are seen, especially along the Luvuvhu, while swarms of redbilled queleas 'flow' through the mopane shrubveld around camp.

The Big Five You may not tick off all of the Big Five, as both rhino and lion can be difficult to find. However, these are more than compensated for by impressive elephant and buffalo herds, which are a sight in themselves. Leopard are commonly seen in the area.

Birds Specials such as white-crowned lapwing, Böhm's and mottled spinetail, narina trogon, tropical boubou and black-throated wattleeye occur.

Don't miss!

One of the highlights is the guided drives to **Crook's Corner** and along the Pafuri, where you'll pass through a forest of large fever trees. If you're lucky, you may even see the elusive Pel's fishing owl.

Activities
Game drives and guided bushwalks are provided according to your requirements. In addition, guided trips to **Crook's Corner**, the fascinating **Thulamela** archaeological site as well as an excursion to **Makuleke Village**.

SINGITA LEBOMBO AND SINGITA SWENI (SINGITA CONCESSION)

SINGITA LEBOMBO
AND SINGITA SWENI
Tel 021-683-3424, Fax 021-671-6776
E-mail: reservations@singita.com
Website: www.singita.com

Orpen Gate 66 km	Lebombo and Sweni ★		
			Mini bar

When it comes to international tourism awards, Singita is no stranger – their flagship, the trés chic Singita of Sabi Sand fame, has scooped many prestigious trophies including best lodge … twice. And, it's only a matter of time before Singita Lebombo and Sweni, the two elemental lodges occupying this concession in Kruger – due east of Satara – step onto the winner's rostrum.

It is not only the chic architecture, ingenious use of natural materials and opulent indulgence of the lodges that make this concession special, however. Rather, it's the concession itself; 15 000 ha of heaven in the lap of the rolling Lebombo Mountains. And, for

The use of natural materials at Singita Lebombo belies its opulence.

those who have vision – which the owners clearly do – you'll immediately realise that, with fences falling, Singita Lebombo and Sweni will soon be located in the heart of the Greater Limpopo Transfrontier Park.

Accommodation
Singita Lebombo perches on a craggy granitic krans overlooking the Nwanetsi River. This location has strongly influenced the design of Lebombo's modern, stylish suites – constructed almost entirely of glass and cane with elements of drystone walling and raw wood. The architects wished to capture the essence of this cliff-edge site and clues for the design have been drawn from eyries, dens and nests. Inside, the rooms are modern and simply, overtly luxurious.
Singita Sweni is located on the banks of the Sweni River in the valley below. Although Singita Sweni lacks the eyrie-inspiring views, it follows the design of Singita Lebombo, taking in sweeping riverside views instead; the rooms are equally opulent.

Both lodges utilise the central spa and 'shopping district'. Here you can indulge in any number of different treat-

Singita Lebombo and Sweni both have 25m pools for training.

ments or simply attempt to regain your waistline on the treadmill. Alternatively, simply grab a coffee, taste an inspired collection of superlative South African wines, purchase gifts and curios (including some magnificent sculptures) or surf the Internet until it's time to venture out in search of wildlife once more.

Wildlife

The camp From your room or the comfortable communal lounge, you can spot a range of birds and animals at the river below. Baboons have learnt to raid the mini-bars of careless guests who leave their rooms unlocked, but aside from their nuisance value, they provide plenty of entertainment as they move through the camps.

The surroundings The concession occupies a range of habitats and environments that ensure you see a diverse range of game, including all members of the Big Five, zebra, wildebeest, giraffe and waterbuck. The guides are extremely knowledgeable and excellent at finding awesome sightings.

The Big Five All members are present,

although rhino can be tricky to spot. The concession is home to black rhino, but these are usually seen only while on bushwalks.

Birds The diverse habitats make this an exciting birding destination. In particular look out for African fish eagle fishing in the waters below the lodge. Also watch the cliffs and rocky ledges for the plethora of swifts, swallows and martins.

On the open grassy areas look for grassland species such as coqui and Shelley's francolin, harlequin quail, red-crested korhaan, black-bellied and kori bustard, secretarybird and others. The entire concession is good for raptors, including vultures.

Don't miss!

Be sure to sleep under the stars on the comfortable mattress provided, protected only by a mosquito net on your balcony.

Activities

Morning and evening game drives are at the discretion of visitors. Guided bushwalks are also available and are tailored to your requirements.

> While snoozing on my deck, I noticed a shadow move in my room – a baboon had quietly pulled the large glass door open and raided my bar fridge. As soon as I sat up, another individual, who was staring down at me from the roof, sounded the alarm and the thief scampered away … an amazing display of teamwork resulting in a bag of nuts as reward.

IMBALI, HAMILTON'S AND HOYO HOYO LODGES (MLUWATI CONCESSION)

No matter which of the Three Cities lodges gracing this attractive 10 000 ha concession you choose, you are in for a memorable experience. The open grasslands of the Mluwati Concession, situated to the southwest of Satara on the Kruger–Manyaleti Private Reserve border, teem with life. Large herds of grazers are common, which, inevitably, are followed by an impressive entourage of predators. Game drives here are never without incident, and you are sure to see lion, zebra, wildebeest, giraffe, elephant and more.

Hamilton's, a camp with a 1900s explorer style, overlooks a small but busy water hole.

IMBALI, HAMILTON'S AND HOYO HOYO LODGES
Tel 031-310-6900
Toll-free 086-100-0333
E-mail: ceres@threecities.co.za
Website: www.threecities.co.za

Orpen Gate 40 km | Hamilton's and Hoyo Hoyo ★ Imbali ★★★

Hamilton's and Hoyo Hoyo

Imbali

Accommodation

Imbali Safari Lodge This flagship is constructed along the lines of a traditional bushveld lodge. However, to minimise the impact on the surroundings, many of the large jackalberries have remained in place and grow through the lodge, giving the entire place a wonderful sense of the living bush. Every suite is equipped with its own spa bath – the perfect way to end your day, gazing up at a 'ceiling' lined only with stars while the bubbles gently ease the creases from your body.

Hoyo Hoyo The name *hoyo hoyo* means 'welcome' in Tsonga, and the camp is styled on a traditional Tsonga village, offering visitors a true African welcome in the heart of the Kruger. The 'Tsonga-nouveau' architecture with its tall, conical thatched roofs is comfortable and the relaxed atmosphere of Africa permeates the entire camp.

Hamilton's has all the style and elegance of an explorer's camp of the early 1900s, from 'antique' sterling-silver cutlery to staff who welcome you in song as they carry your luggage to your room.

Due to the intimate nature of both Hamilton's and Hoyo Hoyo, children younger than 12 are not permitted at either, unless the entire lodge is booked. Imbali has more communal areas and an electric fence, making it more child-friendly and they accommodate children gladly.

All lodges operate on a butler service so there are no mini-bars or coffee

Expect luxury as standard, such as outside spa baths at Imbali Safari Lodge.

winter, a diverse collection of animals is attracted to the thick riverine bush. Baboons and vervet monkeys move noisily along the tree tops, while bushbuck pick through the dense bushes surrounding the decks.

The surroundings Zebra, wildebeest and buffalo herds crisscross the concession which, in turn, attracts large numbers of predators. A large lion pride patrols the area and leopard are common along the river courses.

The Big Five Although rhino can be difficult to find, the rangers are experienced and you have every chance of seeing the Big Five in the area.

Birds This is a great area to see many typical grassland species such as various francolins and spurfowl, harlequin quail, monotonous and flappet lark, red-crested korhaan, black-bellied and kori bustard and others.

stations in your room – if you want something, simply pick up the phone. Neither Hamilton's nor Hoyo Hoyo has outside telecommunications, so they are the perfect escape from the pressures of work.

If you need to remain in contact with the outside world, stay at Imbali.

Wildlife

The camp All three lodges are cleverly situated in different locations on the concession, and have been built so that they leave only the smallest footprint on the landscape. This means that trees grow through decks and the whole space is, quite literally, alive. All three are situated on river courses and although these are generally dry in the

Don't miss!

A midnight spa bath by starlight at Imbali is something not to be missed.

Activities

Game drives are scheduled at visitors' convenience, while walks can be arranged when required. The friendly and efficient team at Imbali gladly hosts small conferences (24 delegates), team-building events and bush indabas.

RHINO WALKING SAFARIS (MUTLUMUVI CONCESSION)

This 12 000 ha concession has been designated a wilderness area within Kruger and, as such, is uncluttered with roads and other human encroachment. This also means that it is in pristine condition and is ideal to explore on foot. The concession is geared to walking safaris, and guests – especially those staying at Plains Camp, which functions as a base for walking operations – tend to walk every morning and evening, unless they want to relax in their rooms.

For those less inclined towards walking, Rhino Walking Safaris has rights to use the roads surrounding their concession for game drives and visitors staying at Rhino Post Safari Lodge enjoy the best of both worlds. They are able to tailor their walking and driving requirements to suit their needs.

Elephants regularly visit the water hole overlooked by Rhino Post Lodge.

RHINO WALKING SAFARIS
Tel 011-467-1886, Fax 011-467-4758
E-mail: info@rws.co.za
Website: www.rws.co.za

Paul Kruger Gate 35 km

Rhino Post

Mini bar

Plains Camp

Rhino Post ★★
Plains Camp ★
Sleepout Deck (not advisable)

Accommodation

Rhino Walking Safaris revolve around two comfortable 'lodges' and a slightly more rustic tree-top 'camp site' – tents set on elevated platforms.

Rhino Post Lodge functions as the base of operations. This comfortable 16-bed lodge, constructed from natural stone, wood, thatch and canvas, sits on the banks of the Mutlumuvi River, which flows only intermittently during the wet season. Tamboti and jackalberry trees grow through the decks and walkways, providing a shady retreat from which you can watch the comings and goings of animals to a nearby water hole between game drives and walks.

Plains Camp is smaller and accommodates eight guests in luxury, en-suite safari tents styled on those of a 19th-century explorer. It is attractively sited overlooking the grassy Timbitene Plain across which herds of zebra and buffalo regularly 'migrate' in search of water. Plains Camp functions as the principal base for walking operations and from here guests venture out on morning and evening walks, led by two experienced, armed trail guides.

Sleepout Decks There is also the option to walk to a set of decks, high in the trees overlooking a small reservoir and drinking trough. The decks offer tree-top camping. Four two-person tents accommodate eight guests on comfortable camping mattresses with sleeping bags.

Game animals wander beneath the wooden structures, seemingly oblivious to your presence and you have the option, weather permitting, to sleep out under the stars protected only by the mosquito-proof netting. Your guides prepare traditional South African meals on an open fire to appease your well-earned appetite, completing your real African camping experience.

Wildlife

In camp All three camps provide fantastic opportunities to see passing wildlife in this game-rich section of the park, among them lion, elephant, buffalo, zebra, giraffe and more. Birds, including brown-headed parrot and African green pigeon among others, are prolific due to the majestic trees that literally grow through the camps.

The surroundings An exciting diversity of habitats and proximity of good water make this a great concession for general game – although, if you focus your activities on walking, sightings can be scarcer. That said, the bushwalking experience is for the discerning guest who craves a more intense, sensual experience than a fleeting motorised visit affords. Smells, sounds, tastes, sightings and tracking (reading the signs of the wild) all take on far more significance when you are on foot surrounded by wildlife. This, combined with the possibilities offered by driving out on some of the Kruger roads – especially after the rest camp gates

have closed – offers visitors the best of both worlds.

The Big Five All of the Big Five are well represented on the concession and you have great opportunities to approach them on foot, which is an altogether different experience to viewing them from within the confines of a vehicle.

Birds Walking safaris provide you with a great opportunity to see grassland species such as coqui francolin, harlequin quail, kurrichane buttonquail, black coucal, and others that can be difficult to spot from a vehicle. Also, it is often possible to get close to kills, which attract a range of vultures and other raptors such kites, as tawny eagles and bateleur, making for great, if often gory, viewing.

Don't miss!

An evening at the Sleepout Decks, combined with the walk in and out, could well be the highlight of any African journey.

Activities

Guided morning and evening walks and game drives are available and are tailored to guests' requirements.

Plains Camp is styled on a 19th-century explorer's camp.

Unfortunately, the park rules prohibit children younger than 12 years from participating in walks, so youngsters cannot be accommodated at Plains Camp or the Sleepout Decks, as these are principally geared towards walking.

TINGA LEGENDS AND TINGA NARINA (JAKKALSBESSIE CONCESSION)

Tinga Legends and Tinga Narina occupy some of the best game-viewing real estate anywhere in Kruger … if not in the whole of Southern Africa. The 5 000 ha concession straddles the Sabie River north of Skukuza, where both wild dog and black rhino sightings have become frequent. You need not venture far from your personal deck or the comfortable communal lounges in order to see fantastic game either. Elephant drink practically every day in the river below, hippo wallow nearby, monkeys cry out alarmed by the passing of one of the resident leopards … And, if this menagerie is not enough, then you can enjoy game drives with the knowledgeable guides in open safari vehicles on the roads surrounding the concession.

The proximity of the Paul Kruger Gate also makes Tinga well within striking distance of Johannesburg.

TINGA LEGENDS AND TINGA NARINA
Tel 0861-TINGA-1 or 013-735-5722
E-mail: reservations@tinga.co.za
Website: www.tinga.co.za

Paul Kruger Gate 22 km

Tinga Legends ★ ★ ★
Tinga Narina ★ ★

Mini bar

Tinga Narina sits on the banks of the Sabie.

Accommodation

Each lodge can accommodate 18 guests in nine luxurious suites, complete with private plunge pools overlooking the river, outdoor showers, fireplaces, mini-bar/fridge and air conditioning. There are satellite TVs and DVDs (with a small library at reception) in all the suites. Children are welcome, although preferably at Legends, which has slightly more communal space and is fenced.

Wildlife

In camp Elephant often drink from the river and are easily viewed in comfort from the lodge. In the pools below the lodge, numerous hippo and crocodile laze about. Leopard have been seen from the camp chasing and catching vervet monkeys. The magnificent jackalberry and sycamore figs lining the river teem with birdlife, including various flycatchers and weavers, African green pigeon, Cape batis, brown-headed parrot, purple-crested turaco and more. In the evening the calls of owls, nightjars and hyenas can often be heard.

The surroundings The entire river course of the Sabie River is densely populated with game and Tinga is no exception. The area surrounding the lodges is good for general game; kudu, impala, giraffe, steenbok, bushbuck and waterbuck are common. Away from the river, zebra and wildebeest are practically guaranteed. Wild dog are often seen in the early mornings. Lizards and snakes, including puffadders, are fairly common. These reptiles attract foraging ground hornbills.

The Big Five Lion, leopard, elephant and buffalo are regularly seen on game drives. Rhino can be harder to spot, but your ranger can always head further south if you keep missing them.

Birds Depending on the areas accessed on your safari drives you can see a diversity of different birds. The lodges overlook the Sabie River with great views of various water birds such as goliath heron, saddle-billed and yellow-billed stork, African fish eagle, hamerkop, pied, giant and malachite kingfisher, while rarer birds such as white-backed night heron, bittern and others may also put in an appearance. Martial eagle is quite commonly seen in the big trees.

Don't miss!

Wallow away the afternoon heat in your personal plunge pool, while keeping an eye out for passing wildlife on the nearby river.

Activities

Drives are undertaken to suit visitors, but typically these follow a morning and evening/night schedule. Guided bushwalks are arranged to suit visitors' specific requirements.

Visitors at private lodges enjoy guided game drives in open safari vehicles.

JOCK SAFARI LODGE (PRIVATE CONCESSION)

The theme of this luxury lodge, situated on a magnificent 6 000 ha concession in the southern region of the park, is the irrepressible character Jock – Sir Percy Fitzpatrick's famous dog and character in his classic book *Jock of the Bushveld*. A sculpture of Jock functions as the lodge centrepiece, while even the delightful 'dog-bone' biscuits served with afternoon tea are in keeping with the theme. The lodge is at the confluence of the Mitomeni and Biyamiti rivers and all rooms have a river view (although both rivers are usually dry).

JOCK SAFARI LODGE
Tel 041-407-1000, Fax 041-407-1001
E-mail: reservations@mantiscollection.com
Website: www.jocksafarilodge.com

Malelane Gate
30 km

★★½

Mini bar

That said, elephant regularly dig for water within a stone's throw of guests as they swill their evening cocktails in the bar. The concession is littered with beautiful granite koppies that form the perfect backdrop to your safari, some of which are worth investigating for their rock art.

Accommodation

The lodge consists of 12 luxury suites, all with personal plunge pools and a covered outside sitting area overlooking the river where you can relax during the heat of the day while keeping an eye on the comings and goings ... or write memoirs of your own for that matter. Each suite is private and your only disturbance is the incessant chattering of the tapestry of life, which wraps the lodge in its magic.

Wildlife

The camp Vervet monkeys race through the trees and birdlife is prolific, including dusky and southern black flycatchers, red-capped (Natal) robin-chat and black-crowned tchagra, among others.

The surroundings A family of ground hornbill lives in the concession and are regularly seen. General game is good and kudu, waterbuck, giraffe, bushbuck, zebra and wildebeest are common.

The Big Five Lion are common, and elephant and rhino sightings are virtually guaranteed, although you'll have to venture out on foot if you wish to see black rhino. Buffalo and leopard can be less common but are usually spotted by most guests.

Birds Sightings are good year round but especially in summer, when migrants, such as various species of cuckoo, swallow and swift, carmine bee-eater, broadbilled roller, woodland kingfisher and steppe eagle return. Ground hornbill are regulars as are many of the grassland species not easily seen from the road, including coqui francolin, flappet lark, kurrichane buttonquail, harlequin quail and others.

Don't miss!

Many of the koppies contain rock art and these are well worth a visit. Sundowners on one of the granite koppies are also highly recommended.

Activities

The routine is casual and an activity schedule is based on your requirements, be that relaxing in the chill room, morning drives, evening drives, walks, romantic picnics and so on. The typical rhythm of the place is a morning drive, followed by breakfast, then for the more energetic a bushwalk fol-

Jock Safari Lodge is located at the confluence of two streams.

lowed by lunch. Usually, there is a little chill time before high tea, an evening game drive and finally dinner.

LUKIMBI SAFARI LODGE (LWAKAHLE PRIVATE CONCESSION)

Situated within the 15 000 ha Lwakahle Concession, bordering on the Crocodile River in the south of the park, this 32-bed lodge offers visitors an intimate bush experience far from the stresses of city life. The lodge itself is well sited on the banks of the Lwakahle River, which flows in the wet season, and game is often viewed from the comfort of your deck chair. Possibly the lodge's strongest feature is the low density of visitors in a relatively large area. The lodge welcomes children, organises activities for them and provides baby-sitters, for a small fee, if required.

> **LUKIMBI SAFARI LODGE**
> Tel 011-431-1120, Fax 011-431-3597
> E-mail: info@lukimbi.com
> Website: www.lukimbi.com
>
> Crocodile Bridge 35 km
> Malelane Gate 22 km
>
> ♿ ★
>
> ❋ 🍳 📺 💃 🍸 Mini bar

Accommodation

Each of the 14 luxurious double rooms has a lounge and magnificent en-suite bathroom overlooking the river linked with lovely natural wood walkways; the two executive suites are complete with their own pool, dining area, guest bathroom and small lounge. All the suites are private, allowing you to share the intimate embrace of the bushveld surroundings with someone special, as the sounds of Africa lull you to sleep.

Wildlife

The camp In summer, the birdlife surrounding the camp is prolific. Numerous owls frequent the area and, at night, the lodge is alive with their calls. Impala

> ### THE LUKIMBI LEGEND
>
> A *lukimbi* is a mythical creature – half owl and half lion. The story goes that Toto, hearing screams from the river, rushed down to investigate. To his horror, he found his betrothed Ntombi being dragged into the river by Mbisi, the crocodile. Toto rushed into the water to rescue Ntombi and a wild tussle ensued … all day the battle raged. One moment the momentum swung towards wily Mbisi, the next towards the brave Toto. Eventually, Mbisi relented and Toto dragged Ntombi up onto the bank and the two lay there in each other's arms bleeding and exhausted – the end was near.
>
> The Great Nkulunkulu looked down on them from the heavens and took pity on the lovers. He gave them new life, and converted them into half owls and half lions – or *lukimbis* – so that they may safeguard other travellers in the bushveld. With the wisdom of owls and the courage and strength of lions, *lukimbis* are there for all travellers who find themselves in peril....

Fresh towels are provided for bathers at Lukimbi's swimming pool.

graze on the small bits of lawn, unperturbed by the camp and its visitors.

The surroundings The area is famous for white rhino, which are regularly seen on game drives. Black rhino tend to be more aloof, but are occasionally encountered on bushwalks.

The Big Five Lion, leopard, buffalo, elephant and rhino are all frequently seen while driving and walking.

Birds If you are an avid birder get the rangers to tailor their drives to ensure you see the maximum number of species. In camp, look for the blue waxbills, and a variety of sunbirds, which flit about probing for nectar. African scops, barred, pearl-spotted and white-faced owl are also often seen and heard. Grassland birds such as various francolin and spurfowl, harlequin quail and kurrichane buttonquail are often seen on drives and walks. The elusive narina trogon and other exciting forest birds are sometimes seen in the dense riverine vegetation.

Don't miss!
The walks are not to be missed. This is your best chance of encountering the elusive black rhino. To encounter one of these ill-tempered beasts on foot is both special and exhilarating.

Activities
Guided morning and evening drives and walks are included in the price. However, management is flexible and will try to accommodate your interests – be they photography, birding, quiet time with a loved one – where possible. Between drives you can utilise the small gym or enjoy some pampering; facials and massages need to be booked a day in advance, however.

The Lukimbi team welcomes function bookings and this is an ideal venue for exclusive weddings, conferences and other special occasions.

Children are particularly well catered for and they will find themselves painting ostrich-shell necklaces, making plaster casts of game spoor near the lodge and more.

SHISHANGENI, CAMP SHAWU AND CAMP SHONGA (MPANAMANA CONCESSION)

Another Three Cities operation, child-friendly Shishangeni and smaller satellite camps, Shonga and Shawu – are located on the 15 000 ha Mpanamana Concession in the southeastern corner of the park, near Crocodile Bridge.

SHISHANGENI, CAMP SHAWU AND CAMP SHONGA
Tel 031-310-6900 or 086-100-0333
E-mail: ceres@threecities.co.za
Website: www.threecities.co.za

Crocodile
Bridge 14 km

Shishangeni Lodge

Mini bar

Camp Shawu and Camp Shonga

Mini bar

Shishangeni ★ ★
Camp Shawu and Shonga ★

The concession is particularly diverse, straddling the Lebombo Mountains and the game-rich plains to the west. This ensures that visitors are practically guaranteed fantastic wildlife sightings in the company of the lodges' well-qualified guides.

The concession is renowned for wild dog, which often breed on the property, as well as both black and white rhino. The concession also falls within the home range of currently one of the largest lion prides in the park, which is often seen on game drives.

Accommodation

Shishangeni Lodge This 22-room luxury lodge is the flagship of the property, offering guests ultimate comfort. The attractive thatched buildings are tucked away in the thick riverine vegetation lining the banks of the Crocodile River and are linked by wooden boardwalks. Each room has all the modern conveniences associated with a five-star lodge, including wonderful outside showers and cosy fireplaces ideal to fend off the winter chill.

Camp Shawu has five units made from elegant, yet rustic materials including canvas, thatch and mud and occupies a magnificent setting on the banks of the Mpanamana Dam. Each room has a private viewing deck, while the comfortable communal area has a swimming pool, bar and comfortable lounge area. There are no telephones here to spoil your perfect escape from the urban jungle.

Camp Shonga This intimate camp accommodates 10 people in five double thatch-and-canvas units raised on wooden platforms. These have private viewing decks with fans and are linked to the communal area with its comfortable lounge, bar and swimming pool by wooden walkways.

Wildlife

The camp Shishangeni Lodge and its satellite camps are situated in diverse habitats. The lodge itself is located within thick woodland along the Crocodile

The luxurious suites at Lukimbi are designed for privacy.

River making it ideal birding territory (see below). Game, such as bushbuck, impala and warthog wander through camp and leopard are not uncommon. Camp Shawu is located on the banks of the Mpanamana Dam and guests can watch hippo and crocodile – not to mention a host of other animals such as elephant, kudu and impala – as they come down to drink, from the comfort of their deck chairs. Cheetah and leopard are regular visitors, and a cheetah kill was recorded in camp during construction. Camp Shonga is situated on a small stream in the rolling Lebombo Mountains. Kudu, impala and bushbuck often wander through camp and white rhino are seen from the decks.

The surroundings You name it, the Mpanamana Concession's got it. In the northern areas typical plains game such as zebra and wildebeest as well as giraffe are common, and it is in this area that one of the largest lion prides in Kruger operates. Generally, game such as impala, kudu, bushbuck and warthog, to name a few, are prolific. Predators, too, are abundant and you are likely to see wild dog on the early morning game drives. Cheetah are also commonly seen in the concession.

The Big Five Both black and white rhino occur in the area, although to see black rhino you need to take one of the bushwalks. Lion, leopard, buffalo and elephant are almost guaranteed.

Birds A number of interesting species occur in this the southeastern border of the park. In particular look out for yellow-rumped tinkerbird (golden-rumped tinkerbarbet), black-bellied starling and purple-banded sunbird, which occur only in this region of the park. Other interesting species include ground hornbill, while the entire concession is good for raptors, including martial and tawny eagle, and bateleur.

Don't miss!

This concession is home to Duke – possibly the world's largest living 'tusker' – so keep a lookout for this very special elephant. Wild dog frequently den on the property.

Activities

Game drives, including night drives and morning and evening walks are offered. Small conferences can be accommodated at Shishangeni.

26 What to do

Sleepover hides, guided walking trails, 4x4 adventure trails … you name it. Under the new dispensation, SANParks has begun diversifying visitor attractions with a range of exciting activities allowing you to experience the park from a completely different perspective, whether you're a first-time visitor or have driven the roads for years.

Guided walking trails offer visitors more intimate encounters with the bush.

SLEEPOVER HIDES

Two hides have been converted into sleepover hides, allowing you to spend an evening in the bush while enjoying the safety and comfort of a hide. They are equipped with fold-down beds, mattresses, bed linen and basic cutlery and crockery. Basic toilet facilities are provided and a small fenced-in lapa area behind the hides means you can enjoy the evening around an open fire in safety. You may only book the facilities en bloc and for a maximum of one night. One drawback, however, is that you can take occupancy of the hide only 30 minutes before gate closing time and you have to be out 30 minutes after gate opening, which could be a problem in summer, unless you are an early riser.

Sable Hide

Overlooking the Sable Dam east of the Phalaborwa Gate, the hide can only be booked at the Phalaborwa Gate and sleeps a maximum of nine.

Shipandani Hide

Sited on the Pioneer Dam near Mopani Rest Camp, Shipandani can be booked through central reservations or from Mopani; guests who have already booked in at Mopani will receive a discounted rate. The hide sleeps a maximum of six.

WALKING TRAILS

There is more to Kruger than simple sightings of the Big Five as they saunter past your car windows. The Kruger National Park is home to myriad organisms all tied together in a finely tuned network creating the natural savanna ecosystems encompassed within its

> **POTATO BUSH**
>
> If you are lucky enough to walk through the park on one of the wilderness trails or guided day walks, you will encounter a new world of smells.
>
> One of the most striking is that of the potato bush (*Phyllanthus reticulatus*), which smells exactly like mashed potato. Potato bush is usually a small shrub or tree that reaches up to 10 m in height, although on occasion it may climb into trees in dense riverine habitats. The smell is most noticeable in the early morning and late evening.
>
> The bush produces small, round, red-black berries in dense clusters from October to December. Birds and game eat the fruit, even although they appear to be poisonous. Traditionally, the leaves and berries were used to treat sores and burns.

Sable overnight hide near Phalaborwa Gate overlooks the Sable Dam.

Shipandani Hide offers fold-down beds, an outside braai area, crockery and cutlery.

WALKING RULES TO REMEMBER

- You can walk only in the company of an approved field guide or ranger from a SANParks camp or private lodge.
- Wear neutral-coloured clothing, avoiding light and bright colours.
- Good walking shoes or preferably boots are a must as the terrain is rough in places.
- Use deodorant sparingly and try to avoid scents and perfume entirely. Natural or scent-free cosmetics are best.
- Walk quietly in single file – speaking alerts game and frightens it away. Click your fingers to attract attention.
- Do not run (unless, of course, you can outrun your buddy...).
- Use insect repellent and high-factor sunscreen.
- Wearing a hat is advisable.
- Take binoculars.

borders. Most of these pass unnoticed by the vast majority of visitors – and not through any fault of theirs. These delicate interactions along the food chain, and the smaller plants and animals, are invisible from the confines of vehicles. To appreciate them fully, you need to venture out on foot.

Guided morning and afternoon bush walks are available from most of the park rest camps, and all of the private concessions – **Rhino Walking Safaris**, in particular, makes walking the focus of activities in their concession (one of the only areas in the park designated as true wilderness).

SANParks also offers seven overnight wilderness trails (see overleaf) with SANParks rangers specially trained for this demanding and interactive activity. All these operate in roughly the same manner.

A maximum of eight guests – from 12 to 60 years of age – are accommodated

Guided walking trails offer a unique opportunity to touch, taste and smell the park.

at a central base camp, from where they are guided by two expert trails guides, usually in the morning, returning to camp during the heat of the day and then setting out in the afternoon again. You are not restricted to the camp area, however, as walkers may be driven to the start of the walking trail each day.

Two groups (of four days and three nights each) are accommodated each week. Participants meet at the designated main rest camp (see individual entries) and are then transported in an open-sided vehicle to the base camp. These are all comfortable but rustic, at remote locations within special landscapes throughout the park. Trails are, to a certain degree, tailored to guest requirements, and although you don't have to be exceptionally fit, you should at least be 'walking fit' – the average morning walk is a slow 12 km.

Afternoon walks are generally shorter.

No trails operate in December and January, because of the intense heat the park experiences during this mid-summer period.

All meals and cooldrinks are included in the price, although participants must supply their own alcoholic drinks and snacks for the duration of the visit.

Wolhuter Trail

Situated between Berg-en-Dal and Pretoriuskop in the special floral reserve in the southwest of the park, this trails camp offers guests fantastic scenery, interesting plants and exciting game-viewing. The area is 'thick' with white rhino, which are often seen on foot. The area is also one of the few places in the park where you can see mountain reedbuck. Visitors meet their guide at Berg-en-Dal.

Bushman Trail

Although this trail is situated close to the Wolhuter Trail base camp (see previous page) and shares a common scenic backdrop, the two trails have very different feels. Activities at Bushman Trail are focused on the fascinating array of rock art found in the south-western regions of Kruger. Of course, animals are not forsaken in the quest for art. Meet at Berg-en-Dal.

Napi Trail

Situated near the confluence of the Napi and Biyamiti rivers, this camp is also sited in a botanically diverse region in the south of the park. White rhino are commonly seen on walks from here, as are zebra and wildebeest. Occasionally, lion, elephant and even black rhino are to be seen too. The scenery is dotted with picturesque granite koppies and numerous rocky outcrops, which add a

Keep quiet on a walking trail; talking frightens off the animals you're trying to see.

dramatic backdrop to the walks. Guests join their guide at Pretoriuskop.

Olifants Backpacking Trail

Located to the south of the Olifants River, near its confluence with the Letaba, this camp occupies one of the most spectacular sites in Kruger, with large rocky outcrops, the spectacular Olifants Gorge and majestic river views. Great sightings of hippo and crocodile are guaranteed, while birders are often rewarded with Pel's fishing owl. The groups assemble at Letaba.

Metsi-Metsi Trail

Metsi-Metsi, northeast of Tshokwane Picnic Site, straddles the park's game-rich eastern plains and the rocky Lebombo Mountain ecozones. Good game sightings are a certainty and if it's your desire to walk with the Big Five, then this is the place to do it! Zebra, wildebeest, kudu and giraffe are common, while, if you're lucky, you could see lion, leopard, rhino and cheetah. You will have good elephant sightings too. Guests meet at Skukuza.

Sweni Trail

Departing from Satara rest camp, this trail heads for the open grassy plains of the legendary N'wanetsi area, close up to the Lebombo range. When the large herds of grazers congregate here, you'll more likely be dodging game than looking for it. The trails camp looks across the Sweni River to a busy waterhole.

Nyalaland Trail

This trail, in the botanically diverse

Trails camps, such as on the Metsi-Metsi Trail, are a basic yet comfortable base.

sandveld of Kruger's northern region, will appeal more to the botanically inclined. Many plants are rare and endemic, such as the sesame tree. The trail is based close to the Luvuvhu River and is probably the best way to experience the prolific birdlife of the Pafuri region, especially towards summer when migrants (rollers, bee-eaters, kingfishers, cuckoos) return. Mottled spinetail, Pel's fishing owl, crowned eagle and African finfoot are possible. Guests join their guide at Punda Maria.

4X4 ROUTES

For those interested in a slightly more adventurous holiday, the park offers visitors with their own 4x4 vehicles the opportunity of undertaking either a one-day adventure trail or the well-established five-day Lebombo Mountain 4x4 trail through the park.

There are four off-road trail routes allowing you to escape the normal tourist routes and explore the back end of beyond. Each one-day excursion is booked at the nearest camp or gate on the day of your trip – no pre-booking is possible. Six vehicles are allowed on each route each day, although the routes can be closed at any time if conditions are unsafe or when driving on the route will harm the environment. This is particularly problematic in the summer rainy season when the routes are impassable after heavy thundershowers.

The park recommends that vehicles are equipped with a GPS, cellphone (there is good coverage over all the routes), first-aid kit, fire extinguisher (you pass through fields of long grass that catch in your radiator, so beware), rubbish bag and at least five litres of drinking water. There are no ablutions or other facilities en route.

While you are on the route, certain restrictions are relaxed and you are permitted to alight from your vehicle (at your own risk), but be careful and aware of animals at all times. Further, you should not stray more than 10 m from your vehicle at any stage.

You should leave no later than 11h00 to ensure you make it back before the gates close. Although the routes are not demanding in terms of off-road driving, your vehicle must be equipped with low range in order to negotiate one or two tricky sections without doing too much damage to the environment. If you get stuck, do not leave your vehicle. A ranger will be dispatched to help once you do not report back to camp in the evening – although this could be only the next morning (other-

Adventure trails require a 4x4, but are not overly challenging.

wise they wouldn't call it 'adventure', now, would they…).

Madlabantu Adventure Trail (Pretoriuskop)

The Madlabantu ('man-eater') trail circles Pretoriuskop in the southwest of the park, using a combination of off-road paths and standard visitor roads to take adventurers through the tall grass plains typical of the Pretoriuskop sourveld. The trail begins from the Fayi Loop, and heads south to the Nsikazi River, which it then follows until this links up with the H2-2 (Voortrekker Road), whereafter you take normal roads north to a second section of off-road track beginning near the beautiful granite koppie on the S10 north of Pretoriuskop. The two halves of the route are very different: in the south you face nothing more challenging than a farm track passing through undu-

lating grasslands, while in the north there are one or two tricky dongas that require more care.

The route passes through some of the largest concentrations of white rhino in the park, so keep a sharp lookout. You may also encounter reedbuck, sable, lion, wild dog, elephant and buffalo.

Mananga Adventure Trail (Satara)

Mananga, meaning 'wilderness', is an apt description of this trail, which passes through the game-rich plains northeast of Satara. The trail itself is not much of a challenge and the trickiest parts entail crossing a small drift that is simple to say the least. Of course, this allows you to truly appreciate the beauty of this knobthorn- and marula-studded savanna ecozone. In particular, look out for giraffe, steenbok, wildebeest, zebra, cheetah, lion and sable as you meander along the flat grasslands.

Northern Plains Adventure Trail (Punda Maria/Shingwedzi)

This trail, the northernmost off-road route in Kruger, passes through wide open grassy terrain northeast of Punda Maria Camp. This gives way to the shrub mopane further north and the trail ends along a mopane-lined avenue dotted with majestic old baobabs. The only human intrusion in the area, aside from the path you are following, are the electricity pylons carrying power from the Cahora Bassa hydro-electric scheme in Mozambique. Look out for wild dog, nyala, Sharpe's grysbok, buffalo, elephant and zebra along the route.

Ever wondered what's beyond the no-entry signs? Book an adventure trail.

Nonokani Adventure Trail (Phalaborwa Gate)

The Nonokani route, which means 'drive slowly', meanders through pretty, mixed mopane/bushwillow vegetation towards the Reënvoel Dam south of Phalaborwa Gate. It then continues all the way south to the banks of the Olifants River before turning north, eventually ending at the busy Sable Dam. Look out for eland, sable, white rhino, buffalo and elephant. This trail was temporarily closed in early 2009.

Lebombo Eco 4x4 Trail

This five-day trail begins at Crocodile Bridge and heads north, covering some 500 km as it winds its way along the Lebombo Mountains, mostly along or close to the Mozambique border, ending in Pafuri. Departures are on Sunday mornings from Crocodile Bridge and participants are requested to meet their guides (who drive their own SANParks vehicles) at 09h00. The trail takes four nights and five days, finishing at Pafuri Picnic Spot at approximately 13h00.

Five four-wheel-drive vehicles are allowed on the trail at any one time, each carrying a maximum of four people. Each vehicle and its occupants should be completely self-reliant as the trail is self-catered (see opposite for a list of recommended equipment). To maintain the wilderness feeling as far as possible, there are no facilities at camp sites, with the exception of two portable toilets.

Three camps are visited on the trail north (Lower Sabie, Olifants and Shingwedzi), where you can refuel, shower and stock up on a few essentials before continuing to your camp site in the wilds.

As you drive, your guide will make regular stops in order to explain a little more about the environment through which you are passing and facilitate your understanding of the bush. This is not a diabolical off-road route and is no test of your 4x4 skills. Rather it is aimed at true nature lovers who hanker after a little wilderness to call their own … even if it is only for a while.

For bookings contact SANParks on phone 012-426-5117 or e-mail hestherv@parks-sa.co.za. No children younger than 12 years old are allowed on the trails. If you require accommodation at the beginning or end of the trail you must book this separately with central reservations – see page 14.

EQUIPMENT CHECKLIST

- Tent, tent pegs and hammer, or rooftop tent
- Groundsheet, rake, spade and broom
- Sleeping bags, towels and pillows
- Inflatable mattress and pump
- 1 gas/paraffin lamp
- 2 litres of paraffin (for a paraffin lamp)
- 2 torches (with extra batteries)
- Folding table and chairs
- Gas stove/cooker, handy braai and gas bottle (x2)
- 3-legged braai stand and grid
- Wood (please supply own)
- 2 x 25-litre water containers
- Refrigerator or cool box (for ice and meat)
- Cooking pot and kettle
- Medium-sized plastic bowl for washing dishes
- Fire extinguisher
- Insect repellent
- Tablecloth
- Washcloth and drying cloth
- Pot scourer and dishwashing liquid
- Refuse bags
- Toilet paper
- Cutlery and crockery
- Mugs and glasses
- Wooden spoon, can opener, egg lifter and cutting knife
- Paper towels
- Carving board
- Hot-water flask

TAKE THESE TOOLS...

- All the necessary spanners, sockets and so on
- Gas utility spares and mantles

GPS waypoints, provided on adventure trails, guide you when the route is indistinct.

FIRST-AID KIT

- Personal medication
- Antihistamine ointment and tablets
- Eye drops
- Paracetamol
- Insect repellant and spray such as Stingose
- Plasters
- Malaria tablets

BETTER SAFE THAN SORRY...

- Personal toiletries
- Road maps
- Camera
- Film
- Binoculars
- Appropriate clothing
- Hat/cap
- Raincoat
- Reference books (guides to mammals/trees/birds)
- Small plastic bowl for washing
- Sufficient food and beverages (a vehicle fridge is handy)

DAY VISITORS

In recent years, there has been a steady increase in the accommodation available outside the park near the entrance gates. This has resulted in more and more people sleeping outside the park boundaries and making day trips into the park every morning – a process greatly facilitated by the advent of the new Wild Cards. One thing to bear in mind is distance. Often, day visitors pack in too many kilometres and zoom about the place without making the most of the sightings they do come across. It is better to work out shorter routes in densely populated areas of the park.

A number of gates now offer guided walks and drives from the gate for day visitors, so consult the 'Gate facilities' table on page 216 and contact the gate directly for more information on times and availability.

Kruger Gate

The proximity of this gate to the Sabie River makes this a popular choice for day visitors. Good sightings are possible as soon as you enter the gate and it is a short drive to the lush and scenic H4–1 (Skukuza–Lower Sabie Road), which follows the course of the Sabie River eastwards. In addition, the **Nkuhlu Picnic Site** (toilets, gas cookers for hire, chairs and tables, small shop and takeaway) makes an ideal midday stopover. Unfortunately, this route can become very busy and you'll have plenty of company at any sightings.

Another prime route from this gate runs north towards the **Tshokwane Picnic Site** (toilets, gas cookers for

> If you don't have a fridge, here is a good tip for summer. Take two cooler boxes – pack pre-frozen provisions for the first half of the trail in one. Pack the second half's cold things in dry ice and seal the lid with duct tape. It will keep everything frozen for a few days.

hire, chairs and tables, small shop and takeaway). There are special day-visitor facilities at Skukuza, with a pool, small shop, toilets and kitchenette. Gas cookers can be hired. For more routes see 'Best drives' in Skukuza (page 68).

Phabeni and Numbi Gates

These are both relatively close to White River, a popular tourism node outside the park. From either gate it is worth navigating a circular route along the Doispane and Napi roads, using Skukuza Rest Camp (or Skukuza's day visitor facility), which has everything you could need including a restaurant, takeaway, shop, toilets and so on, as your midday stopover. For more routes, see the 'Best drives' in Pretoriuskop (page 55) and Skukuza (page 68).

Malelane and Crocodile Bridge Gates

A popular option for day visitors to the south of the park is to enter at one of these camps and exit at the other, having followed the densely populated Crocodile River Road. Unfortunately, the far bank of the Crocodile River falls outside the park and is heavily farmed so you never really feel that you've found a true wilderness. The

Phabeni Gate is ideal for day visitors, allowing easy access to prime viewing in the south.

game is usually very good, however, which certainly mitigates these feelings somewhat. For more routes, see the 'Best drives' in Crocodile Bridge (page 35) and Malelane (page 45).

Orpen Gate

This gate is very close to prime predator viewing country, and does not have any of the 'edge' effect (i.e. unsightly farmed areas, fences and so on) sometimes associated with other gates. It's excellent for lion, hyena and leopard along the Timbavati River and its tributaries. Wild dog are often present and you are almost guaranteed elephant sightings. The best route is to follow the H7 (Satara Road) into Satara, which has all the facilities you could want for a midday stopover.

For more detailed routes in the area, see the 'Best drives' in Orpen (page 76) and Satara (page 80).

Phalaborwa Gate

Situated as close as it is to the centre of Ba-phalaborwa, this is a very popular day-visitors' area. Unfortunately, good game sightings near the gate can be a little infrequent, although the H9 to Letaba is an attractive drive, passing the Masorini Archaeological Site and various interesting granite koppies that rise up from the surroundings. Furthermore, once you reach the area around Letaba Camp animal sightings certainly improve dramatically, and you are likely to see lion, leopard, elephant, buffalo and others. The Letaba Camp makes an ideal stopover, with one of the most scenically sited restaurants in the park overlooking the Letaba River. For more routes, see the 'Best drives' in Letaba Camp (page 103).

Punda Maria and Pafuri Gates

These gates are not widely used by day visitors, as the north is not overly renowned for quick sightings. That said, Punda Maria is close enough to Thohoyandou to make it a viable access point for visitors coming from there. For detailed routes, see the 'Best drives' in Punda Maria Camp (page 134).

What makes Kruger tick?

"Make the boy interested in natural history if you can. It is better than games." Captain Scott in his last message from the Antarctic to his wife and son (later the famous naturalist Sir Peter Scott)

African jacana (above left) are seen throughout the park near permanent water. This also attracts kudu (above right), which favour denser riverine bush.

27 The lie of the land

Kruger is a vast, nearly prisitine, swathe of Africa encompassing some two million hectares and straddling two climatic regions. Its rocks – the very substrate that underlies many of the patterns of diversity readily observable by astute visitors – date back close to the very beginnings of our planet. The park is home to a diversity of wildlife and the average visitor will not travel far without a memorable sighting ... be it a plant, mammal, bird, insect or reptile.

Above: Baobab near Mopani camp. Below: The view from Thulamela archaeological site.

THE LAND
Geological foundations

The geological history of the Kruger National Park predates the arrival of humans, or that of the dinosaurs ... plants and even bacteria are relatively recent phenomena by comparison. In fact, in order to appreciate fully the park's earliest history, it is necessary to cast your mind back three-and-a-half billion years. The earth was a molten blob surrounded by a thin layer of noxious gases; oxygen was present only in minuscule amounts. The continents, as we know them today, didn't exist.

Syenite intrusions protrude from the landscape at Masorini.

Yet, changes were afoot. In places, the molten surface was beginning to crystallise into the first rocks – granites, such as those found near Pretoriuskop today. Slowly, a crust formed, comprising mobile plates floating on the planet's molten core. Over time, more molten material, rich in minerals, forced its way up from the interior, or mantle, filling cracks (intrusions) in this crust and spilling out onto the surface forming sills (horizontal intrusions) of younger granite varieties – such as the gneisses, which underlie most of the western parts of the park, and gabbro, which is found in a corridor west of Satara and in a patch north of Lower Sabie.

Accelerating forward to a time only 300 million years ago, once again, significant changes were taking place. The planet consisted of one supercontinent called Pangaea, surrounded by oceans teeming with varied life forms. The climate was wet and large rivers carrying eroded sediments streamed across the land. In places, sediments were deposited and over aeons compressed to form sedimentary rocks such as the fossil-rich, coal-bearing Ecca shales, which now form the base of the Delagoa thorn thicket ecozone along the H1-3 south of Satara.

Over the next hundred million years or so, Pangaea disintegrated – first, into two large continents, Laurasia (which included Asia, Europe and North America) and Gondwana (including South America, Africa, Madagascar, India, Antarctica and Australia). Laurasia and Gondwana, in turn, began to split into their contingent continents and, by 65 million years ago, all the continents as we know them today could be clearly distinguished.

The forces involved in these tectonic movements were enormous and were accompanied by tremendous geological instability. Lava flows covered parts of the landscape, capping existing geological formations, much like chocolate sauce poured over ice-cream. Outpourings such as these resulted in the basalt and rhyolite formations along Kruger's eastern boundary.

More significantly, however, the

Rain clouds gather over the Lowveld.

shifting continents dramatically tilted this 'layer cake' of geology. Older layers of the 'cake' were exposed in a series of north–south bands stretching across the Lowveld as the entire landscape tilted under the force.

These were the last major upheavals, however, and the landscape slowly settled down. Then erosion set in. Slowly the landscape was modified, leaving the more resistant bands of rhyolite forming the Lebombo Mountains in the east, the ancient granites forming the southern Malelane Mountains, and black reef quartzites forming the Mpumalanga Escarpment further west.

Rivers cut their lazy courses across the Lowveld, carving the valleys we know today. Over the last few million years, subtle additions to the geological formations were finalised. For eons, winds sweeping over the region carried older coastal sands from the western parts of Southern Africa, depositing them across the northern parts of the park. It is upon these sands that the delicate, species-rich sandveld communities – particularly noticeable around Punda Maria – grow today.

CLIMATE
Climatic changes and Kruger

Mirroring the geological changes over the millennia have been changes in climate, which, in turn, have driven ecosystem changes. The park – and, on a grand scale, Africa as a whole – has seen significantly wetter climates. Some 26 million years ago, Africa was much hotter and wetter than it is today. Forests covered the continent, but as conditions became cooler and drier, the forests began to shrink, until eventually only small fragments remained in the tropics and the continent began to look much like it does today.

Within this major climatic shift, in recent times Kruger has experienced regular, small-scale fluctuations in climate, resulting in slightly wetter and slightly drier periods over a seven- to 10-year cycle. These have a fundamental effect on game numbers in what is now the park, but usually do not affect species composition significantly. In dry years, there was less grazing and, killed by illness and starvation, a gradual decline in grazers and browsers followed. This caused a short-term spike in predator numbers as these opportunists took advantage of the glut of weakened and dead animals. But that quickly diminished, and they too began to decline in numbers. Eventually, the rains returned and the cycle reverted – animal numbers increasing as the remaining individuals revelled in the bountiful resources once more.

Over the last 100 years or so, humans have been gradually increasing quantities of what are termed 'greenhouse gases', significantly changing the way

SAVANNA – THE GRASSLANDS OF HUMAN EVOLUTION

Cooler, drier climates led to an increase in the extent of savanna ecosystems, which are believed to have been instrumental in human evolution. The evidence suggests that around four million years ago our earliest ancestors took to the plains, foregoing the trees, and began to walk upright. Maybe, this was to free up our hands, or possibly it was so we could better see predators – no one really knows. Through the following millennia there is systematic fossil evidence of increasing bipedalism (meaning walking upright on two feet), and increasing brain complexity, leading to the crafting of stone tools and so on. Eventually, a few hundred thousand years ago the first modern humans appeared, wandering the plains of Eastern and Southern Africa.

CROCODILES AND GLOBAL WARMING

The sex of crocodile eggs is not determined at birth, but rather by the temperature the egg is incubated at in its early development stages. This means that factors such as global warming could have serious deleterious effects on crocodiles' continued existence – as a severe skew in the sex ratio could result in reduced reproductive success and, ultimately, extinction. Research into these and other effects of global warming is ongoing.

climates function and leading to a gradual warming of the planet. This has serious implications for a fenced conservation area such as Kruger because climates in the area will change.

Animals currently conserved within its borders are 'trapped' by a ring-fence of human occupation. If the climatic conditions change to levels unsuitable for their continued existence, they will die out. For widespread species, this may not be a problem, as representatives will continue in other locations, but certain rare species with limited distribution ranges could become extinct, unable to migrate to an area of suitable habitat.

Factors affecting the weather in Kruger

Kruger's low altitude, proximity to the Indian Ocean and subtropical location all result in the characteristic balmy winter days and hot, humid summers. Rainfall is driven by the huge weather-producing high-pressure system of the Indian Ocean and movements in the subtropical convergence – essentially a band of low pressure that stretches round the globe in the subtropics.

Summer In summer, the southern hemisphere is tilted towards the sun. The resulting increase in solar radiation warms our subcontinent, causing air to rise (resulting in relatively low atmospheric pressures over the interior), allowing the subtropical band of low pressure to move south.

Warm moist air from the Indian Ocean is drawn in from the Indian Ocean high-pressure cell (very simplistically, air moves from high to low pressure) and this, in combination with the convective processes (rising air caused by heating) over the land, results in rain – usually in the form of the spectacular summer afternoon thundershowers.

Occasionally, tropical cyclones hit the region from the warm waters of the Mozambique Channel and bring massive amounts of rain to the region in a few days. This leads to extensive flooding.

Winter In winter, the southern hemisphere is tilted away from the sun and the interior is relatively cooler, resulting in sinking air and the development of a high-pressure cell over the interior. This brings cold, clear, dry conditions to the interior.

Approximately once a fortnight during the winter, cold fronts passing south across the Cape bring cold, clear conditions to most of the country. In Kruger, however, the passage of these fronts draws moist air from the Indian Ocean into the Lowveld, resulting in windy, overcast conditions. Occasionally, these also result in a light drizzle.

KRUGER'S ECOSYSTEM

Kruger falls entirely within a savanna mixed bushveld ecosystem. The term 'savanna' (of Spanish origin) refers to an area dominated by open grasslands dotted with trees. As climate varies, the ratio of trees to grass fluctuates. This type of ecosystem is not unique to Africa, however, and examples occur in Asia and South America.

In Kruger, within the broad definition of savanna, six further major geological areas occur. These form the basis of 14 of the 16 recorded ecozones currently recognised in the park (riverine ecosystems and the alluvial plains of the far north are not directly related to the underlying rock). These distinct habitats all contain characteristic assemblages of plant species, and, in turn, harbour slightly different collections of animals.

In order to understand why the Kruger landscapes look as they do, it is necessary to understand a little more about the forces that drive ecosystems. Two types of factors shape ecosystems, physical and biological. Physical factors include underlying geology (rocks and soil) and climate (rainfall, temperature and wind). Biological factors include species interactions, such as recruitment (driven by factors such as reproductive success and ability of young to disperse), competition and predation.

> The prevailing winds in the park are from the south-southeast and strongest during early summer. In spring (from August to October) the winds are more variable, often blowing from the northwest; approximately 50 per cent of days in the park are wind free.

The purplepod clusterleaf is easily recognised by its purple, four-winged seeds.

Physical factors

Essentially, physical factors lay a foundation into which potential species can move. Firstly, different geological formations result in different types of soil when they erode. Soils originating from basalt or the gabbro and gneiss intrusions in Kruger are nutrient rich and can support a large amount of plant life, while those originating from granite are sandy, nutrient-poor soils upon which only a limited collection of specially adapted plants can survive. Secondly, climate dictates how much water, sunlight and so on the environment will receive. As we all know, nutrients, water and sunlight are the critical factors allowing plants to grow, and hence form the basis of any ecosystem.

Physical factors are thought to be the reason for large expanses of shrub mopane in the north of the park. Nobody is sure why the mopane takes this form here, or why it does not occur much further south of the Olifants River. One likely reason is that it is being constrained by the thin soil profile and underlying rock layer and cannot tolerate the conditions, be they nutrients, day length, growing season or a combination of growing season and the effects of herbivores. That said, experimental seedlings planted in the

Lower Sabie region are growing well at this stage. How they will develop over time is being closely monitored and, hopefully, may shed light on a few of these mysteries.

Biological factors

Biological interactions are much more difficult to measure and quantify. Even seasoned ecologists do not fully understand the complexities involved in the web of biological interactions that have played out over time, resulting in Kruger's landscapes. One thing is clear, however: it is a privilege to have a park such as Kruger, where relatively natural systems still function. As one ecologist says, it is like a time machine. When you enter the gates of Kruger, you are transported to a bygone age, where animals and plants still follow ancient rhythms, affecting each other in a dynamic web of interactions.

There has been much speculation on the roles different groups of animals play in ecosystem functioning. For instance, it is relatively clear that if you remove grazers from the system, significant changes occur, resulting in an increase in the percentage cover of trees and shrubs. Elephant, too, have a major impact on tree and grass cover. But, what about predators?

Some scientists suggest predators are critical to the functioning of savanna ecosystems such as Kruger and are central to maintaining the herbivore numbers, thereby controlling what is happening to the vegetation. For instance, it has been suggested that grazing herbivores such as zebra and wildebeest congregate on open plains

People often think of the vegetation or ecosystem they see today as the 'correct', stable state, as if changes in this are bad. In reality, no single, stable state exists. Ecosystems are living, dynamic entities undergoing constant, gradual changes over time scales of tens, hundreds, thousands and millions of years.

Herbivores play an important role in what happens to the vegetation in an ecosystem.

so that they are harder to hunt ... in so doing they, in turn, maintain the open plains by preventing shrubs and trees from flourishing in those areas.

Megaherbivores – generally those animals of more than 1 000 kg – have a fundamental role to play, as it is unlikely that predators control their population numbers. Take elephants, for example ... What exactly controls their populations is not clear, but their effects on the landscape are indeed clear. They are primarily responsible for creating space in which other species can thrive. Elephants help create patchy areas of grass and woodland, allowing the continued existence of grazers.

Understanding the past 28

Many accounts of the 'human history' of the park begin with the reserve's proclamation and the characters surrounding this incredible achievement. However, the story is much older than that. Evidence suggests that hominids have inhabited the Lowveld, in what is today the Kruger National Park, for approximately 1,5 million years. And, although there is no evidence of their passing, we can surmise that australopithecines were around some three million years before that.

Early visitors were amazed that lions were never perturbed by their vehicles.

Early Stone Age (from 1,5 million years ago)

The earliest hominids in the region were not modern humans (*Homo sapiens sapiens*) but rather one of our nearest ancestors, *Homo erectus*. They hunted in the park as long ago as 1,5 million years ago, leaving stone tools, piles of bones from now extinct animals – exotic creatures such as mammoths, sabre-toothed cats and short-necked giraffes – and their own skeletons as evidence of their passing. Important *H erectus* sites in the park have been discovered near the Luvuvhu River in the far north and further south near the Letaba and Olifants rivers.

Late Stone Age (40 000 years ago)

By this stage, humans proper (*Homo sapiens*) had evolved and were living in the Lowveld. The first known people – the San (Bushman), or their immediate ancestors – were hunter-gatherers and consisted of bands of nomads who followed the game on their migrations, making the most of spatially and temporally variable resources.

By now tool-making had been greatly refined and evidence suggests that the San were utilising bows with poison arrows for hunting, bone fish-hooks and so on. They were also avid painters, utilising blood, gall, egg white, animal fat, ochre and various other pigments and substances to paint schemes on rocky outcrops using hair from the manes and tails of various antelope species as brushes. Scientists believe that these paintings were not merely a recreational activity or insignificant graffiti but an important part of their religious and spiritual beliefs.

Some 100-plus painting sites left by San hunter-gathers occur in the southwest of the park. Images of animals the San believed possessed spiritual powers, such as the eland (the largest antelope), giraffe, elephant and rhino, abound. Interestingly, however, there are no depictions of domesticated animals or colonial imagery, as there are elsewhere in the country. This has led scientists at the Rock Art Research Institute to believe that the paintings are particularly old – certainly many thousands of years.

Visitors may visit these paintings only while participating on the Bushman Walking Trail (page 161 – book well in advance as it's extremely popular) or while staying at Jock Safari Lodge in the southern region of the park (page 150).

Iron Age (about 2 000 years ago)

By the year AD 200, Nguni-speaking people, originally from West-Central Africa, following the fertile valleys along the Luvuvhu, Limpopo, Shingwedzi, Letaba, Sabie and Crocodile rivers, had begun to filter into the area that would become the park. These people were pastoralists who farmed sorghum and raised cattle.

For many years, the San and Nguni peoples coexisted; evidence suggesting that even as late as the 19th century scattered bands of San existed within the park. The increasing populations of Nguni peoples, however, eventually edged out the San.

Left: Iron-Age artefacts in the museum at Masorini. Right: Thulamela occupies a magisterial location close to the confluence of the Luvuvhu and Limpopo rivers.

Thulamela

Between the 15th and mid-17th century, an offshoot of Great Zimbabwe occupied a citadel in the northern parts of what is now Kruger National Park. It was situated on a hilltop, overlooking the Luvuvhu River near its confluence with the Limpopo. The dry-stone walls were similar to those of Great Zimbabwe and housed an elite of an estimated 1000 people within the royal enclosure, while a further 2000-odd people lived in the surrounding areas.

The inhabitants of Thulamela were avid traders, bartering gold, ivory and even slaves with regional neighbours and Arab traders operating from the seaports on the east coast. Archaeologists have found remains of glass beads, Chinese porcelain dating from the Ming dynasty, imported woven cloths, gold, bronze, copper and iron artefacts and royal gongs from West Africa.

Recently, the site has been the focus of significant interest as archaeologists have undertaken the examination of two skeletons found at the site. And although this in itself is not especially interesting, the archaeological methods utilised are.

At a time when many indigenous cultures are beginning to question the validity of removing their ancestors from their graves, this site became the centre of debate about how the remains should be investigated, while ensuring that the modern descendants' wishes for their ancestors were met. The skeletons of the queen and king of this settlement were exhumed, samples and measurements taken and then the royal couple returned to their resting places in what was a world first for international archaeology.

Masorini archaeological site near Phalaborwa Gate.

Masorini

A 19th-century Iron Age site has also been discovered and 'restored' near the Phalaborwa Gate. Compared to Thulamela, this site is relatively recent and was occupied during the early 1800s by the Mojela people, a sub-group of the baPhalaborwa. They were iron smelters and forgers, producing weapons and tools, which they traded (along with food and ivory products) across the Lowveld and towards the Mozambique coast.

Today, visitors can wander through the site and visit the small on-site museum where details of smelting, farming and the inhabitants' lifestyles are depicted.

Enter the Europeans

The first European known to enter the area was a Dutchman, Francois de Cuiper, who travelled east across the Lebombo mountains from Mozambique (or Portuguese East Africa, as it was known in those days) in 1725. He was attacked by indigenous people at Gomondwane, however, and beat a hasty retreat.

The next European 'character' to appear on the scene was a Portuguese trader named João Albasini, who was instrumental in establishing trade links between Delagoa Bay (Maputo) and the interior. He was an enterprising individual and soon befriended the local chiefs and learned their language, enabling him to deal efficiently with his neighbours. Meanwhile, disgruntled with the British annexation of the Cape in 1806, Dutch settlers, or Voortrekkers, began pushing inland from 1836, claiming new areas and eventually occupying what became the Transvaal (today's Mpumalanga, Gauteng, Limpopo and North West provinces).

In order to sever their relations with the British, the new Boer republic urgently required a trade route to Delagoa Bay. This would allow them much greater freedom, enabling them to avoid British taxes and controls. Louis Trichardt led a small group of trekkers east in search of a suitable route but by the time they met with Albasini, who was already relatively well established, many had succumbed to illnesses including malaria. Nevertheless, a trade route – and freedom – was secure by 1850.

The bad years

No reserves or conservation initiatives existed during most of the early 1800s. An orgy of trophy and subsistence hunt-

WHAT WAS THE RINDERPEST?

Rinderpest was a viral epidemic brought to Africa in 1887 with infected cattle from India destined for the Italian army at Massawa, Eritrea. It spread out of control, affecting huge numbers of domesticated cattle and wild ruminants. By 1896 it had crossed the Zambezi, entering South Africa later that year. A number of futile attempts were made to prevent its march south, but the fences, novel prophylactics, slaughter and even days of prayer had little effect. It had a devastating effect on South African cattle, killing huge numbers. For wildlife, it was virtually the final nail … leaving what was left of the once-great herds, already decimated by hunting, in tatters. A vaccine developed in the 1920s immunised for life and vaccination drives around the world have all but eradicated the disease.

ing by foreign 'white hunters', newly arrived settlers fleeing British rule in the Cape and indigenous people alike left the great herds of the subcontinent wasted. In particular the early Boer republics were largely dependent on a hunting economy and consequently the wildlife in the area experienced terrific hunting pressure. The Lowveld did not escape the pillage.

The discovery of gold at Pilgrim's Rest in 1873 and Barberton in 1884 aggravated the problem, attracting more people into the region. These fortune-seekers were largely restricted to the cooler, higher regions of the escarpment by the malarial death trap of the Lowveld summer – malaria was rife, and sleeping sickness and African horse sickness, or nagana, carried by tsetse flies, plagued intruders. In winter, however, the threat of illness declined and hunting parties began infiltrating the region, accelerating the already alarming decline in wildlife.

To exacerbate the situation, a vicious outbreak of rinderpest swept through the region between 1896 and 1898, destroying buffalo herds and other related species. It is estimated that 75 per cent of domestic cattle succumbed during this period. Ironically, this outbreak led to the disappearance of tsetse fly, which retreated into Mozambique and has not reappeared.

Off to a shaky start

By 1889, it had become clear that an enormous problem was looming and debates had begun in the Volksraad – the government of the then Transvaal Republic – on the idea of some sort of game protection. Ironically, these concerns were not based on any notion of conservation in the conventional sense, but rather on the importance of hunting game to the fledgling economies of the Boer republics.

In 1894, the Transvaal government proclaimed it's first 'government reserve' – the Pongola Reserve – on the Swaziland border. This spurred JL van Wijk, the representative from Krugersdorp, and RK Loveday, representative from Barberton, to propose further 'reserve' areas in the eastern parts of the Republic. After much wrangling and debate, these proposals were eventually accepted and on 26 March 1898 the Sabi Reserve was gazetted. This encompassed 250 000 ha bordered by the Crocodile River in the south and the Sabi (now Sabie) River in the north and stretching east from a rough line through today's Skukuza, Pretoriuskop and Malelane camps to the border with Mozambique (then referred to as Portuguese East Africa). Two custodians, Sergeant Izak Holzhausen, based in Nelspruit, and Corporal Paul Bestbier, based in Komatipoort, were appointed to guard the reserve. Kruger had taken its first 'baby' steps.

Amid a tirade of protest, a further 500 000 ha, the Shingwedzi Reserve, was added to the list of government-protected areas. This was bordered by the Shingwedzi River in the south and the Luvuvhu River in the north and was separated from the Sabi Reserve further south by a mixture of state-owned land and private farms.

Unfortunately, these fledgling reserves soon fell off the government agenda as South Africa became embroiled in conflict. The British, anxious to claim the newly discovered gold fields of the independent Boer republics, began initiating policies that could only culminate in one thing – war. The first shots were fired in 1899.

The only happy consequence of the war was that it brought a young Scottish major (later colonel), James Stevenson-Hamilton, to Africa and the Lowveld in particular. After serving with the 6th Inniskilling Regiment during the war, Major Stevenson-Hamilton accepted the position as warden of the two government reserves. On the afternoon of 25 July 1902 he arrived at the escarpment for the first time.

A new era

Initially Stevenson-Hamilton had no staff under his control, little operating budget, no real authority to enforce any regulations and no specific orders other than the vaguest commission, which went something like, 'travel to the Lowveld

Rock art on Jock's concession in the south of the park.

Jock Safari Lodge's statue commemorating Jock, South Africa's favourite dog.

and take charge of the two reserves there present.'

But Stevenson-Hamilton couldn't have been better suited to the job. He was a strict disciplinarian and natural leader, who came from a long line of land stewards back in his native Scotland. He immediately began writing proposals in order to gain funding with which to employ more staff and set to work stopping poaching. Soon, with a small staff, he had significantly reduced poaching, earning the nickname 'Skukuza' ('he who turns everything upside down') for his efforts.

One of Stevenson-Hamilton's first actions was to reduce the number of predators in the park in order to increase antelope numbers – initially, the reserve aimed to increase stocks of the 'royal' hunting species (mainly antelope) rather than conserve habitats for aesthetic or sound conservation reasons. For many years, lion, leopard, wild dog, cheetah, crocodile and even some raptors were shot on sight. It had the

desired effect and, almost immediately, general game began to proliferate.

This was not the end of Stevenson-Hamilton's problems, however. Landowners and farmers surrounding the reserve were at best sceptical and, more typically, downright hostile to his efforts. Farmers urged the government to reconsider their decision, claiming that the reserves harboured dangerous animals and, worse, were a source of dreaded diseases such as foot-and-mouth, rinderpest and so on, that affect domestic livestock.

Stevenson-Hamilton was unwavering in his determination, however, having fallen deeply in love with the area, and gaining an increasing understanding of the natural systems he had been charged to protect. He negotiated with surrounding landowners, cajoled politicians and, more through force of will than through any great support, made the reserves work.

By 1910, the political and economic climate was changing fast and

Stevenson-Hamilton was quick to realise that, in order to ensure the continued existence of the reserves, he would need to adapt. There was no longer a major importance placed on game as a resource and indeed many people again started to question the validity of the protected areas under his care. But, Stevenson-Hamilton had already begun to perceive that there was a more important destiny for the land.

He had observed with some interest the formation of national parks in the USA for the protection of unique landscapes and environments, so that future generations may enjoy them. At the time, this was a major departure from the protectionist ideologies of the day, which tended to be grounded in the utility of the resource being protected. Furthermore, by 1912 he had begun to change his policies on killing lions and other predators, realising there was more to the ecosystems he was protecting than simply a value for hunting. These were radical ideas for the times, when most people simply considered predators as dangerous vermin.

Stevenson-Hamilton began arguing vociferously for a change of designation for his reserves to that of a national park, realising that this would help ensure the long-term survival of what was turning out to be a unique conservation initiative. In this he had many allies, but once again a war interrupted proceedings. Stevenson-Hamilton asked permission to rejoin his unit, and this granted, headed off to the battlefields of the First World War. Luckily, he survived the conflict and returned to renew his struggles.

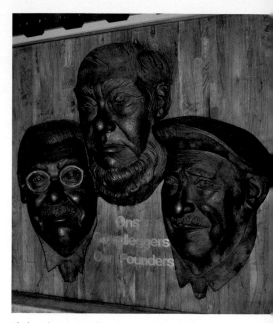

Skukuza's memorial to the park's founders.

The first tourists...

After the First World War, Stevenson-Hamilton returned to the park and his duties. It was not the end of his fight, though. By 1922 things were looking ominous for the reserves. Landowners, mining companies and farmers all urged government to allow them access to the protected areas. However, the minister of lands, Boer War hero Colonel Deneys Reitz, favoured the reserve system and began voicing the need for a national park system in parliament.

On a more positive note, the South African Railways began marketing tours to interesting sites in the Eastern Transvaal. The 'Round-in-Nine' tour took in citrus orchards near Nelspruit, the mountain passes at Pilgrim's Rest and eventually culminated at Lourenço Marques after passing through the

Sabi Reserve. At the time, Stevenson-Hamilton was distressed to note that there were no plans to halt the train in the reserve and, even when he approached the railways, his idea of stopping the train within the reserve was met with derision and indeed laughter. A stop could be arranged, argued the railway officials, if the possibility of a little sport (read "shooting at the wildlife from the train") was available. Stevenson-Hamilton refused, but came away with an agreement that the train would overnight at the siding near Sabi Bridge. Quick to capitalise on the opportunity, Stevenson-Hamilton and his staff organised meals around an open fire in the bush, which proved, to the amazement of the railways, one of the most popular stops for visitors.

In order to capitalise on these positive reports, a ranger began to accompany the train through the reserve, which now passed through during the day so passengers could see game … a relatively novel idea at that stage. The ranger entertained guests and organised walks in the bush at every stop. Tourism within Kruger had begun.

'We'll call it Kruger Park'

With the rise in 1924 of the National Party, the arguments for a national park system came to the fore. Minister of lands, Piet Grobler (a great-grand-nephew of Paul Kruger), vociferously supported the national park concept and is widely credited with suggesting the reserve be called the Kruger National Park – the name appealing to the staunch Afrikaner nationalists.

Finally, on 31 May 1926, the National Parks Act was promulgated in Parliament and the Kruger National Park, encompassing the Sabi and Shing-wedzi reserves, and the areas of land between them, was proclaimed.

'So it's a park … now what?'

The declaration of national park status came as a great relief to all those who had fought so hard for its creation. The park now had a level of legitimacy it never previously enjoyed, making it impossible for government to deproclaim it on a whim. But this didn't mean that Stevenson-Hamilton and his staff's work was over … on the contrary, existing roads needed to be improved, new 'tourist' roads created and rest camps constructed.

By 1927, a circular route around Pretoriuskop was available to outside visitors largely because a rough track between White River and Pretoriuskop existed at that stage. The rest of the reserve was isolated, with no vehicular access possible. The first visitors to the park paid the princely sum of a pound, made their own camps, had to be armed and generally had to fend for themselves within self-constructed thorn barricades at night. During 1927, three vehicles visited the Pretoriuskop area. This increased to 180 in 1928, still restricted to Pretoriuskop. The following year, with more roads completed – it was now possible to travel over most of the area south of the Olifants River – 850 vehicles visited the park.

By 1930, a dozen rest camps, consisting in all of some 100 rondavels, had been built. The modern tourist era in Kruger National Park had begun.

29 Creatures great and small

Impala are often overlooked, which is a pity because they are magnificent creatures. Spend some time watching the herds – you will be amazed by the constant activity.

Whether you're searching for the Big Five, Little Five or Birding Big Six, you'll not find a better place to start your quest than Kruger with its myriad animals, plants and ecosystems. If you're after animals, head for the south. If you're an avid twitcher, head north for the birds. Otherwise just wander about and you're sure to bump into something interesting round the next bend.

MAMMALS

In terms of attracting visitors, mammals are possibly the most important component of Kruger's fauna and flora. No fewer than 147 species occur in the park – some 65 per cent of the mammal species occurring in South Africa. The majority of these are small mammals rarely seen by visitors, as their habits tend to be secretive and many are nocturnal – such as genets, civets, galagos (bushbabies), porcupines, rats and mice. However, large mammal diversity in the park is higher than at any other location in South Africa. This is predominantly because of the size of the area conserved. At nearly two million hectares, this vast area encompasses a variety of different ecozones and spreads across two climatic regions.

Scientists often group mammals according to their feeding strategies – grazers, browsers, carnivores, omnivores and scavengers – in order to discuss the various roles species play in ecosystem functioning. These groupings are not necessarily based on any particular ancestry, however. For example, wild dog and leopard are both carnivores, but they stem from vastly different lineages. Nevertheless, these groupings are valuable as many of the factors affecting a particular feeding group are similar.

CARNIVORES

In the early days of the reserve, rangers considered most predators as dangerous vermin, shooting large numbers of lion, wild dog, leopard, crocodile and others in an effort to increase the number of antelope in the park. Thankfully, this policy did not last and by the 1920s the park was being managed with more consideration to natural ecosystem functioning. These days, predators – and, in particular, the big cats – are the prime tourist drawcards and many visitors are not happy until they've caught even a fleeting glimpse of a leopard, or the tawny flanks of a lion. The best area for predators is generally south of the Olifants River.

The big cats

Lion (***) *Panthera leo* is the largest African carnivore, males weighing 160–250 kg and females 110–180 kg. Population densities of these tawny-flanked cats are highest in the 'lion

ANIMAL STAR RATING SYSTEM

Unlike conventional systems where lions are considered a solid five-star sighting, I have allocated star ratings based on the rarity and special nature of each animal species. You are more than likely to see lions in the park and consequently they get a solid ***.

To get a five-star tick, you'll have to keep your eyes open for a Lichtenstein's hartebeest, suni or something equally rare and exciting.

A cheetah cub – note the striking black 'tear' markings on its face.

triangle', an area running from Olifants to Skukuza to Lower Sabie. Lion are seen without fail in this region.

There is no distinct breeding season, although in Kruger there seems to be a peak in mating from March to July. The male will mount the female every 35 minutes or so over a two- to four-day period, when she is ready. Ritual growling and symbolic neck biting accompany this, which is not aggressive. But don't look away – mating takes only a few seconds and then it's over.

Leopard (****) *Panthera pardus* are widely distributed throughout the park, although you are most likely to see them along river courses – particularly the Sabie, Timbavati, Shingwedzi, Nwaswitsontso and Luvuvhu rivers – where they use the thick riverine bush to stalk prey. You also frequently see them in rocky areas, sunning themselves in the early mornings, surveying their realm. Contrary to popular belief, they are not seen that frequently in trees unless they have dragged a kill into one to prevent it being stolen by hyenas or lions.

Cheetah (****) *Acinonyx jubatus* are the smallest members of the big cats (males 35–65 kg, females 25–55 kg) and occur throughout the park, although you most often see them in the southern and central regions. In particular, look for them between Skukuza and Pretoriuskop and in the Tshokwane, Satara, Kingfisherspruit, Nwanetsi, Lower Sabie and Crocodile Bridge areas. Many people believe that cheetah prefer open areas, possibly because they are depicted in these areas in the media so regularly. In reality, they are as much at home in mixed woodland. They do not, however, occur in forests or woodlands with thick underbrush.

Cheetah are predominantly diurnal, with activity peaks in the early morning

Civettictis civetta are often mistaken for one of the small cats, although they are neither closely related nor share similar habits. In reality, they are closer to the mongoose family ancestrally and are omnivores, relying on a wide range of food, including insects, wild fruits, mice, reptiles, birds, amphibians, millipedes, spiders, scorpions and so on. They are grey-brown in colour with dark spots and bands and usually sport white markings on the face, making them easily recognisable. Occurring widely throughout the park, civets prefer moist savanna habitats with dense woodlands, which supply cover and a sufficient source of fruits and insects – the principal components of their diet. They are predominantly nocturnal with peaks in activity one to two hours after sunset and an hour or so before sunrise. Consequently, your best chance of seeing them is on one of the guided night drives offered by the park. They are rarely seen during the day.

Caracal, as with all of the small cats, are rarely seen by visitors.

caracal (*****) *Felis caracal,* **serval** (*****) *Felis serval* and **African wildcat** (*****) *Felis lybica* are predominantly nocturnal and secretive. This makes them difficult to spot, although on cool, overcast days they are sometimes seen hunting … but this is rare. Caracal and serval are similar sizes, although serval are taller with longer legs and caracal tend to be lower to the ground. African wildcats are slightly larger than domestic cats. Interestingly, domestic cats (first domesticated in 2 000–3 000 BC by the Egyptians, who worshipped them … owners would shave their eyebrows in mourning if the cat died) are descended from these wild cats and can interbreed, producing hybrid offspring.

Other predators

Spotted hyena (***) *Crocuta crocuta* Female spotted hyena are on average heavier than males, largely due to the matriarchal organisation of clans – that is one dominant, or alpha, female rules

and evening, although in cold weather they will sun themselves in the morning, preferring to move when warm, while resting up during the heat of the day.

The small cats

Once the sun has turned in, some of the park's smaller predators head out in search of food. The three 'small cats' the clan. Clans containing up to 18 individuals occupy clearly delineated territories marked by scent, defecating, pasting and scratch marking using glands in their feet.

Once thought of as simple scavengers, hyena are, in reality, efficient hunters when food is scarce. That said, they are able to make use of the entire carcasses they find – skin, bone, hair and even horns. They have powerful jaws designed to crunch through bones and specialised digestive enzymes to digest them, which results in white, powdery scat, rich in calcium.

Hyenas are most active at night and are usually seen in the early morning, late evening or snuffling around the rest-camp fence. They have excellent vision, allowing them to hunt in darkness, and well-developed senses of smell and hearing enable them to detect kills at great distances.

African nights are alive with sounds, of which some of the most distinctive emanate from hyena. They are responsible for a range of whoooops, grunts, cackles, giggles, yells, whines and barks.

Side-striped jackal (*****) *Canis adustus*, a rare member of the Canidae or dog family, is a close relative of the more commonly seen **black-backed jackal** (**) *Canis mesomela*. Side-striped jackals lack the dark, black back and reddish flanks and at a distance appear a dull grey. Close up, however, the side stripe and white tip of the tail are diagnostic. They are slightly larger than their relatives and, unlike black-backed jackals, prefer more densely wooded areas rather than open grasslands.

Wild dogs are seen mostly early in the morning or late in the afternoon.

Hyena scat, easily recognised as it's white when dry, is widely used by tortoises and other small creatures as a source of calcium.

Side-striped jackal are often seen in Kruger in the far northern regions, the combretum woodlands of the southern regions and the tall grasslands surrounding Pretoriuskop, while they are predominantly nocturnal, so look for them in the early morning or at sunset. Black-backed jackal can be seen throughout the park, during the day.

Wild dog (*****) *Lycaon pictus* occur throughout the park in nomadic packs of up to 30 individuals. They are relentless group hunters, repeatedly chasing and attacking their prey – most importantly impala, kudu and waterbuck – until it collapses in exhaustion. Prey is never stalked and the pack will make no effort to make a quick kill as do the big cats.

Adapted to group living, wild dogs show a distinct division of labour, especially during the breeding season.

Hunting members of the pack during this period will return to the den and regurgitate food for the adults that have remained to look after the young and for the young themselves. Because they hunt first thing in the morning or late in the evening, you most often see packs at these times.

Good areas for wild dog include Skukuza, Pretoriuskop, Stolsnek, Malelane, Crocodile Bridge and Kingfisherspruit areas in the south, and between the Sabie River and Tshokwane and also around Punda Maria in the far north of the park. They rely mainly on sight for hunting and so, in these areas, the packs tend to operate in open grassy habitats or open woodlands.

HERBIVORES

Herbivorous species fall into one of two broad categories: grazers or browsers. Grazers concentrate on feeding on grasses and low shrubs while browsers concentrate on the foliage of bushes and trees. Of course, in reality the lines are blurred and many animals will eat a range of plant material. Take elephant as an example – they will eat leaves, grass, fruits, bark and dig for roots and tubers. This generalisation in diet is especially noticeable in times of drought where food resources are scarce. At these times, animals will feed on what they can get. Whereas carnivores tend to feed at longer intervals, herbivores are forced to feed constantly, spending the vast majority of their active hours nibbling away.

Grazers

The largest concentrations of grazers occur in the central plains, especially surrounding Satara. Here large herds of buffalo flow across the landscape, and mixed herds of wildebeest and zebra

Buffalo are grazers, able to digest old grass allowing new growth of sweet, green shoots.

BUFFALO TUBERCULOSIS

African buffalo are closely related to domestic cows and, consequently, many diseases cross easily between the two species. Over the years, this has prompted the construction of strict veterinary cordons surrounding wild buffalo populations to prevent the transmission of nasty diseases such as foot and mouth from buffalo to domestic herds.

These measures, which are strictly enforced, have been relatively successful in preventing outbreaks of disease among domestic cattle. Ironically, the cordon has not protected the buffalo from infections heading the other way.

In 1990, scientists and vets working in the southern areas of the Kruger National Park realised the sudden increase in buffalo illnesses and deaths were largely as a result of bovine tuberculosis or BTB. This is a highly infectious killer, which attacks the lymph nodes, tonsils and lungs and is transmitted between individuals through aerial contamination. It is now believed to infect a significant part of the herd south of the Olifants River, and is slowly moving north every year. A more worrying trend that has been noticed, however, is that lion, leopard and cheetah are also susceptible. They die slow, agonised deaths after contracting the disease from eating infected carcasses.

What is being done? Kruger has an aggressive management plan in place to prevent the disease reaching even greater proportions. A culling programme was initiated to help stem the march of the disease north and testing of new BTB vaccines is ongoing. In addition, there are 'disease-free' breeding herds located in safe areas, including Mapungubwe National Park. These could be reintroduced if the worst-case scenarios play out in Kruger.

---

are common. At first glance, it may seem that grazers all target the same food source and should therefore compete with each other. In reality, each species uses slightly different parts of the same plant resource. Buffalo and white rhino crop tough grasses, while zebra and wildebeest prefer softer, younger shoots. Furthermore, not only is there little competition for the available resources, the presence of other species may indeed be of benefit. On the plains, the more ears and eyes that are on the lookout for predators the better, hence grazers tend to occur in herds. Not only does the chance of detecting a predator increase the larger the herd, but the chance of any one individual being killed is reduced.

One problem faced by grazers is the seasonal nature of their food supply. Grass production is linked to rainfall, and in the dry season food availability is greatly reduced. In order to overcome this, many grazers migrate across the landscape in search of better resources. Possibly the best-known example of this is the great migrations of the Serengeti ecosystem in East Africa, where vast herds of wildebeest and zebra migrate seasonally between Tanzania and Kenya to follow the cycle of rains and new grass growth. The grazers in the Kruger National Park also migrated historically, although these were severely affected first by hunting and farming on the perimeter, then by the construction of the western and eastern boundary fences in 1969. These fences are slowly coming down in places, largely driven by the formation of the Greater Limpopo Transfrontier Park. It is hoped that once all the fences have been removed many species will revert to their old migratory routes.

Buffalo (***) *Syncerus caffer* are the largest pure grazers in the region (eland are larger but have a more generalist diet and will browse leaves and berries, and dig for roots). Males tend to have heavier bosses (the horny plates on their foreheads) and larger horns than females. They occur throughout the park, although they are more prevalent north of Satara. Buffalo prefer grassy areas interspersed with woodlands, which provide adequate shade during the hottest period of the day. Adult bulls (and less often females and juveniles) will also wallow in mud, which further aids thermoregulation and helps to remove skin parasites.

Gregarious in nature, buffalo occur in large herds often numbering into the thousands. These fragment to a certain degree, however, as smaller units make use of isolated food and water supplies. This is more typical during the wet season; in the dry season, the herds tend to remain together and will move large distances in search of food and water.

Waterbuck (**) *Kobus ellipsiprymnus* are always associated with water and rarely seen far from it in the park. Their most striking feature is the large white circle on their rump; males and females differ in the distinctness of this. Males also carry horns.

They are gregarious, usually occurring in small herds that seldom number more than 12, but on occasion herds can be as large as 30. There is a strong

Waterbuck enjoy lush, green grass associated with river courses.

social order – with territorial males, nursery herds and bachelor herds.

Burchell's zebra (*) *Equus quagga* is the only zebra species that occurs in Kruger – and, it must be said, virtually throughout the park, preferring open woodland and grasslands where suitable water is present. You see them mostly on the central plains surrounding Satara and in the eastern areas of the park. They are inclined to move between summer and winter grazing areas – in the wet summer season, zebra obtain their water from pans and temporary sources but as this begins to dry, they revert to their winter grazing areas near permanent water.

Without doubt, zebra are one of the characters of the bushveld and few visitors leave without fond memories of the 'amusing' *kwa-ha-ha* call made by these horses caught in their pyjamas by evolution.

Blue wildebeest (*) *Connochaetes taurinus* are found in most of the park, although north of the Olifants River they tend to occur only in scattered herds. South of this, they are prevalent northeast of Satara, north of Lower Sabie, between Lower Sabie and Crocodile Bridge and near Mlondozi Dam. Small populations also occur to the west of Satara, all the way to Orpen Gate and around Pretoriuskop.

Wildebeest are gregarious, occurring in herds of 20 to 30 individuals, although at times aggregations reach many thousands. In Kruger, most wildebeest do not migrate, largely due to the radical population reductions of the migratory herds after the construction of the western boundary fence in 1969.

William Burchell is probably one of the best-known pioneer naturalists. On his journeys during 1811–12 from the Cape, he first documented stone plants, white rhino, Burchell's zebra, Burchell's coucal and many other species. Upon his return to the United Kingdom, he was met with disbelief. "There can be no such animal!" declared people when he first described a zebra.

White rhinoceros (****) *Ceratotherium simum* are the third largest land mammal in Africa, after elephant and hippo. Males weigh anything from 2 000–2 300 kg, while females are smaller. They are slightly larger than black rhino and have a square jaw, rather than a hooked upper lip, as is the case with black rhino. They are also grazers, whereas black rhino are browsers. Black and white have no bearing on the colour of the animals and in reality both tend to take on the colour of the soil on which they are found through a process of wallowing and dusting.

In Kruger they occur mainly in the south of the park, especially south of the Sabie River – Berg-en-Dal is often called 'the rhino camp' because of the high density of rhino in the area. They prefer flat, open woodland habitats, where there is good grazing, water and shade. Water is important for both drinking and wallowing.

Hippopotamus (*) *Hippopotamus amphibius* are the second largest land mammal on the African continent. They occur in rivers and dams throughout Kruger, with the highest densities in the Olifants River. Appropriately, its

Hippos lazing on the banks of the Limpopo River at Crook's Corner.

English name, hippopotamus, is from the Greek meaning 'water or river horse'. The African name for hippo, *mvuvhu* or *mvubu* is onomatopoeic and based on its grunting call.

Hippo require sufficient open water in which to submerge fully and show a distinct preference for shallow sandy areas near the banks where they can stand. Once a good area is located, hippo will remain in that pool as long as there is sufficient food in the surroundings. They are grazers, feeding on land during the night, but return to the water at sunrise and are rarely outside the water during the day unless the weather is cold. In the water, they generally occur in social groups, consisting either of females with their calves or bachelors. Solitary animals are either territorial bulls or females about to give birth, which occurs in the water. **Eland** *Taurotragus oryx* (***) are the largest antelope species in the park, and occur only in the northern drier regions, particularly north of Olifants Camp and in the Pafuri area. They obtain enough water from their food and they do not rely on water sources.

Although evidence exists from rock paintings that eland existed in the park historically, they were hunted to local extinction in the 1800s. When Stevenson-Hamilton took over as warden, he did not find even one of them. In 1905 he travelled to Portuguese East Africa (Mozambique) and negotiated for two individuals with which to begin restocking Kruger. He returned with a young, 'tame' bull and female calf. These were kept in captivity at Sabi Bridge (Skukuza) and slowly their numbers increased to 10. Unfortunately, however, all but one of these died while Stevenson-Hamilton was away fighting in the First World War.

This loss was less significant than it may have been, however, as by 1920 a small number of eland had migrated into the northern areas of the park from Mozambique and established themselves. Even today, eland are elusive and difficult to find.

The rare antelope

Roan antelope (*****) *Hippotragus equineus* are closely related to sable, which they superficially resemble. They occur in a very restricted range in Kruger, found only in mopane shrubveld and mopane/bushwillow woodlands in the eastern parts adjacent to the Lebombo mountains. They are extremely rare so consider yourself especially lucky if you see any. The population has always been extremely small (around 70 individuals) although during the era of water provision (when boreholes were sunk in dry areas) their numbers briefly peaked at 500. The park is working hard to bolster these numbers, however. Watering points are slowly being decommissioned and two breed-

Lichtenstein's hartebeest are rarely seen in the park.

ing camps – in the Vlakteplaas region near Shingwedzi and the other in the Mooiplaas region near Mopani – have been constructed to exclude predators, allowing roan numbers to increase.

Apart from these two breeding camps, two free-roaming herds occur in the park and members of the largest – situated along the tar road between Punda Maria and Shingwedzi – are sometimes seen.

Sable antelope (*****) *Hippotragus niger* are patchily distributed in the park. They prefer open woodland with adjacent grassland containing medium-high stands of grass; they avoid short grass. They are most likely to be seen in the early morning or late afternoon near Pretoriuskop, along the Hlangelene Road near Manzimhlope and near Phalaborwa Gate.

Herds can number up to 12 in Kruger, although small groups of two to four are more common. There is a strict dominance hierarchy with one dominant male and one or more dominant females; the other members are ranked according to age – juvenile females ranked higher than males. Bachelor herds consisting of non-territorial males occur.

Lichtenstein's hartebeest (*****) *Sigmoceros lichtensteinii* were once widespread through the Lowveld and possibly even extending into the Pongola region, but became locally extinct some time during the mid-1900s. Re-introduced in 1985 to Kruger – from Malawi – they are surviving well in two areas: the grasslands surrounding Pretoriuskop and in the mopane shrubveld near Punda Maria.

Like their more common close relative, the red hartebeest, they are predominantly grazers preferring medium to tall grasses, feeding during the cooler times of the day when the moisture content of their food is highest. This enables them to go several weeks without water but they drink readily when water is available.

Tsessebe (*****) *Damaliscus lunatus* gets the name 'tsessebe' from the Tswana name for the species, *tshêsêbe*. In Kruger they have a restricted distribution, mainly occurring north of the Letaba River – although small herds are sometimes seen near the Mlondozi Dam and in the Pretoriuskop area. They prefer open savanna woodland and avoid over-utilised grassland areas and dense stands of woodland. Their diet includes medium-high grasses and shrubs, while they also enjoy the new grass on recently burnt areas.

Although tsessebe may look ungainly, they are reputedly the fastest antelope in the park. Unfortunately, this speed is often undermined by their curiosity – which borders on stupidity according to one source. They will remain standing in the open, looking inquisitively at the source of a disturbance even after two or three animals have been shot by a hunter. This, possibly, contributed to the rapid decline of the species during the commercial hunting in the 1800s. They remain an endangered species.

Browsers

Browsing opens up many more niches than does grazing – the suite of variables includes the height at which feeding takes place, the type of food

TANNINS – PLANTS DEFENDING THEMSELVES

Plants are not simply helpless victims of herbivory ... they often defend themselves. Physically, some have evolved thorns and other mechanical devices to help protect themselves. Plants have also developed a number of chemical deterrents to prevent overgrazing. These range from poisons to other chemicals such as tannins (your morning tea contains a form of tannin), which retard the efficiency of digestion. However, producing these chemicals can take its toll on the plant, and many have thus developed the ability to increase the concentrations of tannins in their leaves only once an animal begins browsing. If you watch giraffes, for example, you will notice they tend to feed for relatively short periods on one tree before moving off upwind. Scientists have suggested this is due to the food plant's rapid increase in tannin (other scientists disagree, suggesting it is simply a way of lowering the risk of attack by predators). As for the reason why they move upwind – it has been shown that plants can 'communicate' with those nearest them, probably by releasing pheromones – a group of chemicals closely related to hormones. Plants downwind receive the message and begin increasing tannin in anticipation of attack.

sought, ability to deal with plant defences and so on. As a result, more species use this feeding strategy. In Kruger, browsers are widely distributed throughout the park, although some species tend to prefer certain habitat types and therefore slight changes in species composition is noticed as you move between different ecozones.

Impala (*) *Aepyceros melampus* are the most numerous mammals in Kruger, with an estimated 110 000 individuals occurring in suitable habitats throughout the park. They are particularly prevalent along major, permanent watercourses such as the Sabie, Crocodile, and Letaba`rivers.

Avoiding open grasslands, impala are generally found on the edge of wood-

Herds of impala gather in the bush alongside the Sabie River.

Female kudu scan their surroundings for signs of danger with their 'radar' ears.

land where there is suitable cover and water – both essential habitat requirements. Gregarious by nature, they form small herds of six to 20 individuals, which often coalesce into larger aggregations numbering into the hundreds. Within any one aggregation, you are likely to find a complex array of social interactions and groupings. During the rut, there are territorial males (which aggressively defend territories), bachelor herds (consisting of non-territorial or juvenile males) and breeding herds (consisting of ewes and juveniles). In the non-breeding season the interactions relax and the herds mix into loose breeding herds and bachelor herds.

The rut, or mating season, is dramatic. From April to June the landscape resounds with the constant rattle of horns smacking into each other and the roaring of territorial bulls as they threaten would-be competitors.

When alarmed, impala give a loud snort and if spooked will bolt, leaping gracefully over bushes and other obstacles. They are extremely nervous, generally, and usually one or more of the animals in the herd act as lookouts while the others feed. One of the most memorable of all Kruger sightings is seeing a group of these agile buck leaping – cascading – in a graceful arch, over an obstacle when they take fright.

Bushbuck (**) *Tragelaphus scriptus* are closely related to kudu and nyala, although they are significantly smaller. They have a patchy distribution within the park and tend to occur along major river courses, where they frequent dense bush. This makes them difficult to spot. They are generally solitary in nature, although males and females sometimes occur together in loose association and small nursery herds are sometimes seen. They often associate with monkeys and baboons, feeding on fruit, flowers and so on dropped by those species forag-

In order to circulate sufficient blood to their lofty brains, the blood pressure of a giraffe is some two-and-a-half times that of a human. Their cardiac walls are 7 cm thick in order to pump the blood at these high pressures.

ing in the trees above. Bushbuck are selective browsers feeding on a range of food sources including leaves, twigs, fruit and berries. Grass is grazed on occasion. They are water dependent and drink daily.

Kudu (**) *Tragelaphus strepsiceros* are one of the most majestic animals in the park and even obsessive 'Big Fivers' will often pause to marvel at them. Stevenson-Hamilton described them as 'the acme of nature's effort to attain perfection of type'.

Mostly active during the early morning and late afternoon, kudu occur throughout the park's woodland areas, including dense thorn thickets. Male kudus have a particular fondness for dense riverine vegetation lining major rivers, while female kudus tend to be more widespread.

Kudu are gregarious, occurring in small herds that seldom number more than 12 individuals. Outside of the rutting period, which occurs from April to June, males form bachelor herds or join up with female herds. From February to March the incidence of solitary males increases in preparation for the mating season.

A shy species, kudu are constantly on the alert, especially when traversing open countryside or approaching water to drink. The slightest distur-

bance alarms them and they will flee for cover with graceful bounds without looking around to assess the source. In thick vegetation, however, they are less skittish and stare at the source of disturbance, with their radar-like ears 'focused', assessing the danger.

Nyala (**) *Tragelaphus angasii* are closely related to kudu, and are often found grazing alongside female kudu where they coexist and are not easy to tell apart. Males and females have distinct white stripes on their flanks and usually significant white spots on their hind quarters. They are patchily distributed in the park and are most often associated with river courses – especially the Luvuvhu, Shingwedzi and Letaba rivers. They are most common in the north of the park where they were first recorded only in the early 1920s. By the 1980s they were very common in the north, but the drought of the 1990s decimated the species.

Nyala feed mainly at night but are also active in the shade during the day. Small herds of ewes and their young are common, occasionally forming loose aggregations of up to 30 individuals. Bulls tend to be solitary.

Southern giraffe (**) *Giraffa camelopardalis giraffa* males reach 4,9–5,2 m in height while females are slightly shorter at 4,3–4,6 m when fully grown. Although this height has its advantages – allowing them to reach a selection of vegetation unavailable to other browsers – it comes at a cost. Due to the high blood pressure required to pump blood to these heights, they cannot lower their heads to the ground at rest because of the risk of rupturing blood vessels in the brain. In deep sleep, which occurs for a few minutes at a time, the head is bent backwards and rested on the back.

Giraffe occur throughout the park, preferring woodland habitats. They are diurnal and, like most such species, spend the hottest parts of each day resting in the shade. Unlike most other animals, however, giraffe walk with both legs on the same side moving in unison, contributing to their ungainly lope when running.

There is no strong social organisation, although bulls tend to be solitary and females tend to occur in small herds. They are docile in nature, but females with calves will actively defend them if threatened. Males spar by slamming their horns which, unlike those of antelope, are solid bone covered by a thin layer of skin, against the necks of their opponents during mating season. This rarely causes severe injury, although on very rare occasions deaths have been recorded.

African elephant (***) *Loxodonta africana* have shown a remarkable recovery in Kruger since 1902, when Stevenson-Hamilton reported them absent from the newly proclaimed Sabi Reserve. This was largely due to the hunting pressure that had been exerted on elephant in the 200-odd preceding years. It is estimated that in 1903 more than 544 310 kg of ivory was imported into the United Kingdom – at a cost of an estimated 50 000 elephants. These days, Kruger contains too many elephants and park authorities are once again beginning to address their management through a number of strategies

Elephant eat around 200 kg of vegetable matter a day, mainly grass.

(see overleaf). Elephant occur throughout the park, although the highest densities occur along the major rivers of the central area around the Letaba, Olifants, Tsendze, Shingwedzi, Mphongolo and Shisha rivers. Smaller populations occur south of here, along the Sabie, Timbavati, Biyamiti and Crocodile rivers. Females are gregarious, occurring in herds led by a single matriarch and a number of closely related females and their calves. Males leave the herd without provocation and either join up with small bachelor groups or follow a solitary existence – only coming together to court and mate.

Generally, elephant are peaceful and aggressive interactions are rare, although violent battles sometimes occur between males in the presence of females in oestrus. These are often

THE GREAT ELEPHANT DEBATE

The number of elephant in Kruger has grown steadily since the early days of the reserve. Initially, this posed no threat, but by the 1960s researchers in the park had become worried about the effects of elephant on the functioning of the savanna ecosystem through which they roamed; the problem being that elephant modify their environments significantly. If the elephant density is too great, severe habitat degradation occurs – mainly because elephant uproot huge numbers of trees in their quest for food.

One of Kruger's prime goals is to actively conserve biodiversity and, in order to facilitate this, elephant numbers were controlled, by culling, at between 7500 and 8000 – the park's perceived carrying capacity. This was an unpopular solution, however, and animal-rights activists and concerned members were instrumental in having the culling process halted in 1994.

Elephant numbers have ballooned since the moratorium on culling and currently there are 11000-plus in the park. This has spurred numerous discussions on how effectively to deal with the problem. Many people see the transfrontier park programme as a potential solution. Although this has opened up vast areas of territory in neighbouring countries with few or no elephants, the problem is convincing Kruger's elephants to move. Initial attempts at relocation have proved frustratingly unsuccessful, with many of the translocated animals moving back to where they were initially captured. Costs are also prohibitive.

Another mooted solution has been the idea of contraception to control breeding. The drawback, however, is that contraception will only retard population growth and not actively reduce populations.

It seems that in the short term, culling is the only logical approach.

---

devastating, causing destruction to trees and vegetation in the area, and on rare occasion death to one of the suitors. Females seem to promote these competitive interactions by producing loud low-frequency calls, designed to attract potential mates when they enter oestrus. Bulls in musth actively seek out breeding herds with females in oestrus.

Females will also act aggressively in defence of their young. When showing aggressive tendencies – signalled by raising and shaking the head, ears held out, kicking up dust with the forefeet and trumpeting – elephant are extremely dangerous. Swaying or shaking may predict a mock charge. (It's a state of frenzied sexual excitement in males, when a gland between ear and eye secretes a watery fluid.)

If this turns real, the elephant folds back its ears, tucks its trunk behind its jaw and rushes at the intruder with tusks thrust forward. That's the time to get out – fast! Humans and cars have been attacked on rare occasions in the park – usually by bulls in musth!

The small antelope

A number of small antelope, many of which can easily be mistaken for each other, occur in the park. Typically, all the 'small antelope' lead secretive lives and are usually seen only in thick vegetation or tall grass, making good sightings tricky. Of these species, you are most likely to see steenbok and grey duiker. These are both widely distributed and occur throughout Kruger.

Steenbok (***) *Raphicerus campestris* are reddish-brown antelope, with the male carrying a small set of sharp horns 13–19 cm in length. They prefer relatively open areas and are usually solitary or in pairs and are by far the most common and frequently seen of the smaller antelope. They are selective browsers.

Grey duiker (***) *Sylvicapra grimmia* are greyish-brown in colour and should not be confused with steenbok. Males carry a set of short sharp horns 10–18 cm in length. Grey duiker prefer woodland, scrub and bushy habitats and are rarely seen on short grassland. Their name means 'diver' from their habit of diving into thick cover when alarmed. They are browsers.

Red duiker (*****) *Cephalophus*

natalensis are reddish-brown in colour; males carry sharp horns 7–10 cm in length. They are very rarely seen and have a restricted distribution, occurring only in the area around Pretoriuskop, Skukuza and along the Sabie River. They prefer thick vegetation and are found mainly in forests, although within this habitat, they require a range of trees and shrubs that flower and fruit throughout the year. Red duiker are predominantly diurnal.

Oribi (*****) *Ourebia ourebi* could be confused with steenbok, which they superficially resemble, but they are substantially bigger. However, oribi are very rarely seen in the park, occurring in a very restricted area surrounding Pretoriuskop. They prefer open grassland and floodplain, but the presence of cover is important. Males carry horns 8–19 cm in length. They are grazers.

Sharpe's grysbok (*****) *Raphicerus sharpei* are closely related to steenbok, which they resemble, although their reddish-brown coat is speckled with flecks of white. They are also of similar size. Sharpe's grysbok are relatively rare, nocturnal and have a patchy distribution, tending to be absent from the southwest and northeast; densities are highest in the Lebombo mountains south of the Olifants River and the extreme northern areas north of Punda Maria. They tend to be found in bushy areas are browsers.

Suni (Livingstone's antelope) (*****) *Neotragus moschatus* are the smallest antelope, rare and seldom seen. They have a very limited distribution, occurring only on the alluvial plain and Sandveld ecozones east and west

Always scan the koppies and rocky areas for klipspringer.

> Klipspringer have fluid-filled, shock-absorbing pads on their rounded hooves to absorb the impact of landing on hard rocky surfaces.

of Punda Maria. They prefer woodland and forest habitats with dense underbrush, and the thick riverine scrub along rivers. Their peak activity periods are during the morning and evening, but they are active during the day and night. With their reddish-brown coat, they resemble steenbok and Sharpe's grysbok, but are significantly smaller, weighing just 5–6 kg. The males carry a set of sharp horns 7–13 cm in length. They are browsers.

Klipspringer (***) *Oreotragus oreotragus* occur throughout the park, but are generally restricted to rocky outcrops, from whence they get their Afrikaans and common name (meaning 'rock jumper'). They are particularly agile and bound over precipitous drops, using the tiniest of ledges. To achieve this they have specially modified, rounded hooves, enabling them to maintain their footing. They are predominantly diurnal and usually occur in pairs or larger groups consisting of parents with young. They are unmistakable, with a coarse, yellowish-grey coat. The males carry a short set of sharp horns 10–15 cm in length. They are non-specific browsers and eat a range of leaves, fruits and so on. In order to provide additional nutrients, klipspringers chew mud rich in salt and occasionally bones.

Monkeying about…

Five species of primate occur in the park: baboon, vervet monkey, samango monkey, and thick-tailed and lesser galago (bushbaby). Of these, baboon and vervet are commonly seen by visitors during the day and lesser galago at night. Samango monkey are occasionally seen in the Pafuri region along the Luvuvhu River, while thick-tailed galago occur in forested areas north of the Luvuvhu, east of Satara and in the vicinity of Skukuza, Pretoriuskop and Berg-en-Dal.

Chacma baboon (**) *Papio ursinus* are Kruger's largest primates and, with their well-developed, dog-like muzzle, are unmistakable. They are gregarious in nature and occur in large groups, which can number up to 130 individuals under exceptional conditions. Smaller troops of 20 to 30 members are more common. Occasionally, troops overlap but this creates absolute pandemonium, with the dominant males aggressively shaking the branches and screaming, while chasing and herding their females away … needless to say, these groupings do not stay together long.

Baboons and vervet monkeys are easily socialised and have learnt to 'steal' and beg food from humans. They are accustomed to vehicles and climb through any window in search of food if you give them half a chance. If you encounter a baboon troop, do not feed them! Fed individuals become dangerous and eventually the park authorities are forced to kill them. By feeding them, you are simply signing their death warrant.

Vervet monkeys (top) and baboons (above) make fascinating watching.

A wide range of food is eaten, prompting one researcher to quip that it would be easier to list the things not eaten than eaten. Fruits and leaves are enjoyed, as are grasses, bulbs and rhizomes from which they obtain extra water. They also search under stones for insects, scorpions, spiders and will even eat slugs. On rare occasions, the troop will hunt meat and kill small antelope such as young impala or bushbuck and birds such as francolins.

Vervet monkey (**) *Cercopithecus aethiops* are small silvery-grey monkeys found throughout the park. Highest densities occur along river courses where the little black faces peer out at you from the green filigree lining the banks. They are gregarious, occurring in troops numbering up to 20 individuals and more, with a clear order of dominance within the troop. The social structure is maintained by a combination of aggression and threat displays, which take various forms including bobbing, sudden jerky movements and staring while retracting their eyebrows to show the pale area above their eyes and on their eyelids (which contrasts with their black faces). Dominant males may also display their genitals to subordinates by standing in front of them an open-leg stance, although the role of this display is unclear.

Unlike baboons, the species has a less elaborate mating behaviour, associated with the fact that the menstrual cycle is less 'visible.' As with baboons, vervets have learnt to associate humans with easy meals and often mooch through rest camps and picnic sites in search of a quick bite or an open window.

Lesser galago (bushbaby) (***) *Galago moholi* epitomise cute: they weigh just 150–230 g and have large, friendly eyes and big 'ewok' ears. They are strictly nocturnal and, although not common, can be seen on night drives as rhey leap through the trees.

The colloquial name 'bushbaby' stems from their call, which sounds very much like a human infant crying. They are solitary when foraging, but sleep in unrelated groups of six or seven individuals, returning to a nest where members of the group will spend significant time grooming each other. Nests are made from leaves and are placed in dense vegetation, the forks of trees, hollow trees, old birds' nests, roofs or other parts of buildings.

Bushbabies are agile and are able to leap 7 m in a single jump. They also tend to be shy and the most one normally sees of them is two glowing eyes in the trees, which bound away when you shine your light on them.

Smaller critters …

Tree squirrel (*) *Paraxerus cepapi* occur widely in all areas of Kruger where there are suitable trees to provide the necessary shelter and food. They are small and generally solitary, although pairs and small family units consisting of a dominant male, one or two females and their young occur. Mutual grooming, scent marking and the smell of the nest are important group recognition factors. The whole group will mob predators, calling loudly with clicks and high-pitched whistles, accompanied by flicking of their tails.

Squirrels often forage on the ground and their first response to danger is to dash for the trees. They are capable of leaps in excess of 2 m and when alarmed race to the high branches before pausing. They are diurnal and spend most mornings and late afternoons feeding, tending to rest up during the hottest hours of the day. In cooler weather, they may remain active all day.

Scrub hare (***) *Lepus saxatilis* are the most common 'rabbits' in the park. They occur throughout Kruger in all ecozones, but are predominantly nocturnal, although you often see them early in the morning and in the late afternoon. During the day, they lie up in thick cover and may return to the same spot for days while foraging in an area. They feed predominantly on the leaves, stems and rhizomes of grass, preferring green grass, but are able to utilise dry grass if needs be. Generally, they are solitary but if a female is in oestrus she will be attended by one or two males.

Dwarf mongoose (***) *Helogale parvula* are widely distributed throughout the park and are most often found in association with a disused termite mound or large log in which they have made their home. As their name suggests, they are the smallest of the species with a body length of 18–28 cm (tail 14–19 cm). They are strictly diurnal and are most active during the morning and afternoons, although in cold, overcast weather they may not venture out of their burrow, where they huddle together for warmth.

They are social animals, living in tight-knit packs of up to 35 individuals, led by a dominant female. She is the only female that is reproductively active in the pack and all other members will work together to feed and care for the young. The pack forages together, although there are always one or more members posted as sentries. This is a fluid arrangement, however, and sentries will take it in turns to forage with the pack. Their diet consists mainly of insects, but they will take lizards, frogs, mice, spiders, eggs, berries and fruit.

Banded mongoose (***) *Mungos mungo* are gregarious, occurring in packs of up to 50 individuals. They are patchily distributed within the park, occurring within woodlands and scrub thickets where there is suitable cover. They are larger than either the dwarf or slender mongoose, measuring 30–45 cm (body) with a tail of 15–30 cm. They are dark in colour and heavily banded, with 10–12 transverse black bands across their back, which distinguishes the species from the other large mongooses. Typically, banded mongoose are shy and spook easily, dashing into the underbrush as you approach. Consequently, good sightings are rare. All members of the pack are reproductively active, although there is a strict hierarchy. The highest ranked females are mated first and over the next four or five days so are all other females. However, all these females give birth on the same day … with the less dominant individuals having to truncate their gestation as any young not born on the same day as those of the alpha female will be killed by her. Their diet includes insects, lizards, snakes, birds, eggs, spiders, scorpions, berries and fruits.

Warthog (**) *Phacochoerus aethiopicus* occur throughout the park in grass-

Warthog are feisty and often come off on top against predators thanks to their tusks.

land and open woodland habitats. The females tend to occur in small groups, usually consisting of two sows and their piglets, while males are usually solitary. You are most likely to see warthog in the area between Lower Sabie and Crocodile Bridge; near Orpen Gate; around Tshokwane and in the Nwanetsi and Phalaborwa areas. They are also common in the north between the Luvuvhu and Limpopo rivers.

They are diurnal and spend much of their day feeding. This can be highly entertaining as they feed by snuffling along on their elbows, which are protected by thick calluses. Their diet consists predominantly of roots and tubers which they dig up with their snouts, short grass, berries, fruits, carrion, birds, rodents and reptiles.

Characteristically, when they are startled, warthog head for cover with a dainty little trot holding their tails

A saddle-billed stork fishing for frogs near Punda Maria.

straight up in alarm. They are taken by leopard and lion, but are fierce opponents, their tusks inflicting severe wounds. They live mainly in old aard-vark holes.

BIRDS

Most visitors to Kruger focus their attention on finding lion; some take in the rest of the animal kingdom along the way; very few appreciate the wealth of birdlife that exists in the park. This is unfortunate as many slow 'animal days' in Kruger can be significantly bright-ened by watching birds.

Kruger contains a diverse array of habitats and this, combined with its sheer size, makes it arguably the best birding destination in South Africa. Some 507 species occur in the park, a total larger than many small countries. In order to unlock this wealth of birdlife, it is best to have a specialist bird guide, and bird checklists are available in the shops. A reasonably competent birder could expect to see 125 to 250 bird spe-cies over a week or so.

FINDING BIRDS

Birding is more productive in the summer months when migrant species return from their winter breeding grounds. The majority of bird species occur throughout the park. Certain areas, however, tend to contain more species than others. Generally, the south – with its denser vegetation and diversity of habitats – and the far northern region – with the wide flood plains of the Luvuvhu and Limpopo rivers – are the best birding areas.

The open plains surrounding Satara are excellent for typical grassland species, while the riverine forests that line the main rivers contain a host of species more commonly associated with true forests (there are none in the park). Water birds occur throughout the park wherever water bodies occur – marshy areas, artificial water holes, river courses and dams.

Some of the most reward-ing birding can be had in the older rest camps and picnic sites where birds such as hornbills, weavers and glossy starlings have become habituated to humans. Newer bushveld camps in a more natural setting will attract the shyer species.

Kruger is a particularly good area in which to find raptors. Keep an eye on the sky as watching the behaviour of vultures can lead you to kills.

Brown-headed parrot eating coral tree flowers in Berg-en-Dal camp.

REPTILES

Most people cringe when they even hear the word … uuuugghhh, reptile! They are quick to conjure up pictures of bloodthirsty snakes, cold-blooded crocodiles and so on. In reality, the group contains a fascinating array of individuals. Kruger has 114 species of reptile – 58 lizards, 50 snakes, five tortoise/terrapins and one crocodile.

Nile crocodile (**) *Crocodylus niloticus* is, of all the park's reptiles, the one visitors tend to notice most often. They are the biggest reptile in the park by some way; large individuals measuring up to 4 m (yes, that's four metres!) and weighing in at more than 500 kg are relatively common.

Crocodiles are found throughout the park, wherever suitable permanent water bodies exist. Although they eat mainly fish, they are effective hunters, lurking submerged in the shallows for animals to come down to drink. Large individuals are capable of taking anything from small antelope to buffalo. Prey is generally drowned and sometimes stored to facilitate rotting, enabling the crocodile to rip chunks from it more easily.

Snakes

Many people have no great desire to see snakes at any stage in their lives – and a visit to the Kruger National Park is no exception. In reality, however, people who see snakes during their visit can count themselves exceptionally lucky. Generally, snakes are shy of humans and prefer to slide away at the first sign of our presence. Of the 50 species in the park, most visitors will see no more than one or two during their stay. Pythons and puffadders are most commonly seen – not that these are the most abundant snakes in the park, but rather their lethargic behaviour increases your chance of seeing them.

African rock python (*****) *Python sebae natalensis* is the largest snake in Africa and often grows to 5 m. It has a propensity to laze about in sunny spots or to move slowly. Pythons are ambush predators and lurk about on busy game trails or other suitable areas waiting for their prey to pass, even in river pools. They eat almost anything from game birds to impala.

Puffadder (*****) *Bitis arietans* are one of the most poisonous snakes in Africa. They are slow and lazy, reluctant to move and, unlike most other snakes in

Male tree agamas display their bright blue heads in Skukuza.

South Africa, will remain in your path as you approach until eventually, when you get too close, they lash out. They are often seen crossing the roads in Kruger. Occasionally one will slither into camp (notify reception immediately if you are worried by a snake in camp – do not try and remove it yourself).

Lizards

Far and away the most often seen reptiles in the park are geckos. Both **dwarf gecko** (*) *Lygodactylus capensis capensis* and **house gecko** (*) *Hemidactylus mabouia* are found prowling the walls of your room in search of insects. They occur in all rest camps and are well worth watching, especially at night when large numbers of flying insects are attracted to the lights. The geckos will wait nearby, stuck to the walls with specially designed pads on their toes, and in a flash will snaffle anything that ventures too close.

It is also worth wandering through the camps as a number of lizards are found in the trees and rockeries of the camps. **Tree agama** (**) *Agama atricollis* are common; the males have a bright blue head during the breeding season in order to attract potential mates. Unfortunately, the overall number of lizards you are likely to encounter in the park is relatively low because they are not easily spotted from the confines of a car. There are exceptions, however.

The largest species of lizard in the park are **water leguaan** (**) *Varanus niloticus*, which are often seen sunning themselves near rivers and water holes, and **rock leguaan** (***) *Varanus exanthematicus albigularis*, which are mainly terrestrial. These large dinosaur-looking reptiles are voracious predators, and prey on frogs, birds, small mammals and other lizards.

On night drives, the guides often spot **chameleon** (*) *Chamaeleo dilepis dilepis* in the trees in the beam of the searchlight, allowing you to get a good look. During the day, search for their shape as they will have taken on the background colour almost perfectly.

Tortoises and terrapins

Visitors often confuse terrapins with tortoises but, in reality, the distinction is simple as it is based on habitat: tortoises are all terrestrial and terrapins are all found in fresh water. Turtles, the other member of this group of reptiles, are strictly marine.

Two species of tortoise occur in the park, namely **leopard tortoise** (****) *Geochelone pardulis* and **hingedback tortoise** (*****) *Kinixys spekii*. Leopard tortoises are most commonly seen walking in the veld and across the roads. They have a distinct black-and-yellow colour scheme. Hingedback tortoises are rare, found predominantly in the western parts of the park. They are a drab greeny brown and this distinguishes them from leopard tortoises. Both tortoise species are herbivorous and feed on a variety of leaves and grasses.

Three species of terrapin occur in the park: **hinged terrapin** (*) *Pellusios sinuatus*, **Cape terrapin** (****) *Pelomedusa subrufa* and **panhinged terrapin** (*****) *Pellusios subniger*. Hinged terrapins occur in all permanent water holes and rivers in the park and are regularly seen sunning themselves on the banks.

Cape terrapins occur in temporary wetlands and water holes. They hibernate during the dry season in a burrow, which they dig in the mud as the pools dry. Panhinged terrapins are rarely seen.

All species of terrapin are carnivorous, feeding on an array of aquatic life such as fish, frogs, insect larvae and crabs, and scavenge scraps from crocodile kills.

Look out for terrapins in the streams and dams throughout the park.

Kruger at a glance

DISTANCE
Distances between main camps and gates; camps listed in alphabetical order distances are in kilometres.

	Berg-en-Dal	Crocodile Bridge	Letaba	Lower Sabie	Malelane	Mopani	Numbi Gate	Olifants	Orpen Gate
Berg-en-Dal	**	149	234	113	12	281	97	219	213
Crocodile Bridge	149	**	196	34	141	243	130	181	175
Letaba	234	196	**	162	226	47	216	32	117
Lower Sabie	113	34	162	**	105	209	95	147	141
Malelane	12	141	226	105	**	272	94	210	204
Mopani	281	243	47	209	272	**	263	86	164
Numbi Gate	97	130	216	95	94	263	**	201	195
Olifants	219	181	32	147	210	86	201	**	102
Orpen Gate	213	175	117	141	204	164	195	102	**
Pafuri Gate	453	415	218	380	444	172	434	250	335
Paul Kruger Gate	83	88	173	53	74	220	65	158	152
Phabeni Gate	110	115	200	91	102	247	32	185	175
Phalaborwa Gate	285	246	51	213	277	74	267	83	167
Pretoriuskop	92	125	211	90	85	258	9	195	184
Punda Maria	415	377	176	342	408	130	396	212	297
Satara	165	127	69	93	156	116	147	54	48
Shingwedzi	344	306	109	271	333	63	325	141	226
Skukuza	72	77	162	43	64	209	54	147	137

Speed	Time to drive 50 km
20 km/h	2 hr 30 mins
30 km/h	1 hr 40 mins
40 km/h (max on dirt)	1 hr 15 mins
50 km/h (max on tar)	1 hr

	Pafuri Gate	Paul Kruger Gate	Phabeni Gate	Phalaborwa Gate	Pretoriuskop	Punda Maria	Satara	Shingwedzi	Skukuza
Berg-en-Dal	453	83	110	285	92	415	165	344	72
Crocodile Bridge	415	88	115	246	125	377	127	306	77
Letaba	218	173	200	51	211	176	69	109	162
Lower Sabie	380	53	91	213	90	342	93	271	43
Malelane	444	74	102	277	85	408	156	333	64
Mopani	172	220	247	74	258	130	116	63	209
Numbi Gate	434	65	32	267	9	396	147	325	54
Olifants	250	158	185	83	195	212	54	141	147
Orpen Gate	335	152	175	167	184	297	48	226	137
Pafuri Gate	**	392	418	246	438	76	287	109	380
Paul Kruger Gate	392	**	50	224	60	354	104	283	12
Phabeni Gate	418	50	**	251	23	380	131	309	38
Phalaborwa Gate	246	224	251	**	261	201	119	137	213
Pretoriuskop	438	60	23	261	**	389	140	318	49
Punda Maria	76	354	380	201	389	**	245	71	342
Satara	287	104	131	119	140	245	**	178	93
Shingwedzi	109	283	309	137	318	71	178	**	271
Skukuza	380	12	38	213	49	342	93	271	**

REST CAMP FACILITIES

	Petrol	Day visitors	Shop	Gas hire	Public telephone	Camping	Pool	Restaurant	Function/ conference	Cultural site
SANPARKS CAMPS										
Balule Rustic Camp					Y	Y				
Bateleur Bush Camp					Y				Y	
Berg-en-Dal Rest Camp	Y	Y	Y	Y	Y	Y	Y	Y	Y	Y
Biyamiti Bush Camp					Y					
Boulders Bush Lodge										
Crocodile Bridge Complex	Y	Y	Y	Y	Y	Y				
Letaba Rest Camp	Y	Y	Y	Y	Y	Y	Y	Y	Y	Y
Lower Sabie Rest Camp	Y	Y	Y	Y	Y	Y	Y	Y		
Malelane Satellite Camp					Y	Y				
Maroela Satellite Camp					Y	Y				
Mopani Rest Camp	Y	Y	Y	Y	Y		Y	Y	Y	
Olifants Rest Camp	Y	Y	Y	Y	Y		Y	Y		
Orpen Gate Complex	Y	Y	Y	Y	Y					
Pretoriuskop Rest Camp	Y	Y	Y	Y	Y	Y	Y	Y		
Punda Maria Rest Camp	Y	Y	Y	Y	Y	Y	Y	Y		
Roodewal Bush Camp										
Satara Rest Camp	Y	Y	Y	Y	Y	Y	Y	Y		
Shingwedzi Rest Camp	Y	Y	Y	Y	Y	Y	Y	Y	Y	
Sirheni Bush Camp					Y					
Skukuza Rest Camp	Y	Y	Y	Y	Y	Y	Y	Y	Y	Y
Talamiti Bush Camp					Y					
Tamboti Tented Camp					Y					

PRIVATE LODGE FACILITIES

	Pool	Restaurant	Function/ conference	Cultural site	Gym	Children <12	Telephone
PRIVATE LODGES							
Hamilton's	Y	Y					
Hoyo Hoyo	Y	Y					
Imbali Lodge	Y	Y	Y	Y		Y	Y
Jock Safari Lodge	Y	Y	Y	Y		Y	Y
Lukimbi Safari Lodge	Y	Y	Y		Y	Y	Y
Pafuri Tented Camp	Y	Y	Y	Y			
Rhino Post Lodge	Y	Y	Y		Y	Y	Y
Rhino Walking Safari's Plains Camp	Y	Y					
Rhino Walking Safari's Sleepout Decks							
Singita Lebombo Lodge	Y	Y	Y		Y	Y	Y
Singita Sweni Lodge	Y	Y	Y		Y	Y	Y
Shishangeni Lodge	Y	Y	Y			Y	Y
Shawu Camp	Y	Y					
Shonga Camp	Y						
Tinga Legends	Y	Y	Y			Y	Y
Tinga Narina	Y	Y					Y
The Outpost Lodge	Y	Y	Y			Y	Y

Gate	Telephone	Route
Pafuri Gate	013-735-5574	N1 past Louis Trichardt, turning right onto the R525 before Musina (Messina)
Punda Maria Gate	013-735-6870	N1 to Louis Trichardt, R524 to Punda Maria
Phalaborwa Gate	013-735-3549	N1 to Polokwane (Pietersburg), R71 to Ba-Phalaborwa via Tzaneen
Orpen Gate	013-735-0237	N4 to Belfast, R540 to Lydenburg via Dullstroom, R36 and R531 to Orpen via Ohrigstad, JG Strijdom Tunnel and Klaserie
Paul Kruger Gate	013-735-5107	N4 to Nelspruit, R40 to Hazyview, turn right to gate. N4 to Belfast, R540 to Lydenburg via Dullstroom, R37 to Sabie, R536 to Hazyview continuing to the gate.
Phabeni Gate	013-735-5890	N4 to Nelspruit, R40 to Hazyview, turn right to gate. N4 to Belfast, R540 to Lydenburg via Dullstroom, R37 to Sabie, R536 to Hazyview continuing to the gate.
Numbi Gate	013-735-5133	N4 to Nelspruit, R40 to White River, R538/R539 to Numbi Gate
Malelane Gate	013-735-6152	N4 via Witbank and Nelspruit to Malelane
Crocodile Bridge Gate	013-735-6012	N4 via Witbank and Nelspruit to Komatipoort

* N = normal; D = disabled

Distance from Johannesburg	Petrol	Toilets	Shop	Picnic	Public tel	Guided drives for day visitors
600km		N			Y	
550km		N			Y	
490km		N	Y	Y	Y	Y
434km	Y	N	Y	Y	Y	
460km 470km		N&D	Y		Y	Y
430km 440km		N&D				Y
411km		N&D			Y	
428km		N&D			Y	Y
475km	Y	N&D	Y	Y	Y	Y

	OPEN		CLOSE
	Park gate	Camp gate	Park and camp
January	05h30	04h30	18h30
February	05h30	05h30	18h30
March	05h30	05h30	18h00
April	06h00	06h00	18h00
May–July	06h00	06h00	17h30
August	06h00	06h00	18h00
September	06h00	06h00	18h00
October	05h30	05h30	18h00
November	05h30	04h30	18h30
December	05h30	04h30	18h30

PARK RULES

• Visitors must remain in their vehicles unless in designated areas.
• The maximum speed limit on tar roads is 50 km/h and 40 km/h on dirt roads. This is strictly enforced and trapping is common.
• Gate times are strictly adhered to and arriving back in camp after the gates close incurs stiff penalties.
• All firearms must be declared on arrival at the gate so they can be sealed.
• Overnight visitors are allowed to stay only in recognised and designated overnight facilities such as rest camps and sleepover hides.
• All accommodation units and camp sites can be occupied from 12h00 and must be vacated by 09h00.
• No pets are allowed.
• Open vehicles are allowed into the park only with the appropriate permits.
• Do not feed any animal – perpetrators will be fined.
• Do not get out of your vehicle – perpetrators will be fined.
• Cellphones may be used only in camp and in cases of emergency, otherwise they should be switched off or to silent on game drives.

USEFUL CONTACTS

GENERAL
Kruger Mpumalanga Airport
013-753-7500
Compass Game Park Services
011-802-7200
Optica Phototechnical Repair Service
(White River) 013-750-0554,
e-mail: zdenek@telkomsa.net

AIRLINES
**South African Airlink central
reservations** 011-978-1111;
Kruger Mpumalanga Airport
013-750-2531/2/3/4
**South African Airways Central
Reservations** 0861-359-7222

MEDICAL
Malaria Hotline 082-234-1800
Netcare Travel Clinic Johannesburg
011-807-3132; Pretoria 012-344-0110;
Cape Town 021-419-3172;
Durban 031-303-2423;
Port Elizabeth 041-374-7471

WILD CARD
www.sanparks.org, or tel
086-123-4002

SANPARKS

EMERGENCY CALL CENTRE
013-735-4325

RESERVATIONS
Central reservations
012-428-9111, fax 012-343-0905,
e-mail: reservations@sanparks.org,
website: www.sanparks.org
Head office 012-426-5000,
e-mail: info@sanparks.org,
website: www.sanparks.org
Conference facilities
013-428-5086, 012-343-0905,
fax 012-426-5488,
e-mail: traveltrade@sanparks.org
Lebombo Eco 4x4 Trail
012-426-5117,
e-mail: hestherv@sanparks.org

SATELLITE OFFICES
Johannesburg: 011-678-8870
Cape Town: 021-426-4260
Durban: 031-304-4934
Nelspruit: 013-755-1988

SKUKUZA
Golf course 013-735-5543
Nursery 013-735-4312
Doctor 013-735-5638
Airport (private transfers only, no
scheduled flights) 013-735-4251
First National Bank 013-735-5632
Post Office 013-735-4313
Selati Grill 013-735-5658
Avis at Skukuza 013-735-5651
Skukuza surgery 013-735-5638

USEFUL CONTACTS

CAMPS

Balule 013-735-6306
Bateleur 013-735-6843
Berg-en-Dal 013-735-6106/7
Biyamiti 013-735-6171
Crocodile Bridge 013-735-6012
Letaba 013-735-6636
Lower Sabie 013-735-6056/7
Malelane 013-735-6152
Maroela see Orpen Camp
Mopani 013-735-6535/6
Olifants 013-735-6606/7
Orpen 013-735-6355
Pretoriuskop 013-735-5128
Punda Maria 013-735-6873
Roodewal see Satara Camp
Satara 013-735-6306/7
Shimuwini 013-735-6683
Shingwedzi 013-735-6806
Sirheni 013-735-6860
Skukuza 013-735-4000
Talamati 013-735-6343
Tamboti see Orpen Camp

GATES

Crocodile Bridge 013-735-6012
Malelane 013-735-6152
Numbi 013-735-5133
Orpen 013-735-6355
Pafuri Gate 013-735-5574
Parfuri border 013-753-5757
Paul Kruger 013-735-5107
Phabeni 013-735-5890
Phalaborwa 013-735-6509
Punda Maria 013-735-6870

PRIVATE CONCESSIONS

Hamilton's, Hoyo Hoyo Tshonga Lodge and Imbali Safari Lodge 031-310-6900, fax 031-307-5247, toll free 086-100-0333, e-mail: ceres@threecities.co.za, website: www.threecities.co.za

Jock Safari Lodge 041-407-1000, fax 041-407-1001, e-mail: reservations@jocksafarilodge.com, website: www.jocksafarilodge.com

Lukimbi Safari Lodge 011-431-1120, fax 011-431-3597, e-mail: info@lukimbi.com, website: www.lukimbi.com

Mpanamana Concession Shishangeni, Shawu & Shonga 031-310-6900, fax 031-307-5247, toll free 086-100-0333, e-mail: ceres@threecities.co.za, website: www.threecities.co.za

The Outpost 011-245-5704 or 086-636-5364, e-mail: theoutpost@mix.co.za, website: www.theoutpost.co.za

Pafuri Camp 011-257-5111, fax 011-807-2110, email: enquiry@wilderness.co.za, website: www.wilderness-safaris.com

Rhino Walking Safaris 011-467-1886, fax 011-467-4758, e-mail: info@rws.co.za, website: www.rws.co.za

Singita Lebombo and Sweni 021-683-3424, fax 021-683-3502, e-mail: reservations@singita.co.za, website: www.singita.co.za

Tinga Private Game Lodge 013-735-5722 or 0861-TINGA-1, e-mail: reservations@tinga.co.za, website: www.tinga.co.za

RECOMMENDED READING & CAMP MAP ICONS

Jock of the Bushveld
by Sir Percy Fitzpatrick, Jonathan Ball
Publishers, 1986.

*South African Eden: The Kruger
National Park*
an autobiography by James Stevenson-
Hamilton, Struik, 1993.

*Pocket Photoguide to Mammals of
Southern Africa*
by Burger Cillié, Sunbird Publishing, 2004.

*Getaway Guide to Where to Watch
Game in the Kruger National Park*
by Nigel Dennis, Sunbird Publishing, 2000.

Pocket-guide to Southern African Birds
by Burger Cillié & Ulrich Oberprieler,
Sunbird Publishing, 2002.

*Robert's Birds of Southern Africa
7th Edition*
edited by Gordon Maclean, John Voelcker
Bird Book Fund, 1993.

Kruger National Park
a social and political history of the park
by Jane Carruthers, University of Natal
Press, Pietermaritzburg, 1995.

*A Dictionary of the Kruger National
Park Place Names*
by Hans Bornman and JJ Kloppers, SAN-
Parks, 2005.

Kruger National Park – A History
by Dr Solomon Joubert, SANParks, 2007.

CAMP MAP KEY

Entrance Gate · First Aid · Wheelchair · Petrol · Mechanic · Carwash · Museum · Library

Post Office · ATM/Bank · Telephone · Television · Air-con · Laundry · Shop · Restaurant

Conference Facilities · Eco Info · Bar · Picnic Facilities · Gym · Swimming Pool

INDEX